Life and Death

A collection of classic poetry and prose

INTRODUCED BY
Philip Pullman

EDITED BY
Kate Agnew

Published in the UK in 2004 by Wizard Books,
an imprint of Icon Books Ltd., The Old Dairy,
Brook Road, Thriplow, Cambridge SG8 7RG
email: wizard@iconbooks.co.uk
www.iconbooks.co.uk/wizard

Reprinted in 2007

Sold in the UK, Europe, South Africa and Asia by
Faber and Faber Ltd., 3 Queen Square, London WC1N 3AU
or their agents

Distributed in the UK, Europe, South Africa and Asia by
TBS Ltd., TBS Distribution Centre, Colchester Road,
Frating Green, Colchester CO7 7DW

Published in Australia in 2004 by Allen & Unwin Pty. Ltd.,
PO Box 8500, 83 Alexander Street, Crows Nest, NSW 2065

Distributed in Canada by Penguin Books Canada,
90 Eglinton Avenue East, Suite 700, Toronto, Ontario M4P 2Y3

This edition published in the USA in 2007 by Totem Books
Inquiries to Icon Books Ltd., The Old Dairy,
Brook Road, Thriplow, Cambridge SG8 7RG

Distributed to the trade in the USA by National Book
Network Inc., 4720 Boston Way, Lanham, Maryland 20706

ISBN-10: 1-84046-567-0
ISBN-13: 978-1840465-67-9

Typesetting by Wayzgoose

Printed in the UK by CPI Bookmarque, Croydon, CR0 4TD

Kate Agnew read English at the University of Oxford, has chaired the Children's Booksellers Association and has served as a judge for the Smarties Prize and the Whitbread Award. She was a contributor to the *Cambridge Guide to Children's Books* and co-wrote *Children at War* with Geoff Fox. In 1999 she won a special British Book Award for her contribution to the National Year of Reading.

Philip Pullman has won many awards for his children's books, including the Carnegie Medal, the *Guardian* Award, the Smarties Prize, and, most recently, the Whitbread Book of the Year Award for *The Amber Spyglass*. His acclaimed fantasy trilogy, *His Dark Materials*, comprising *Northern Lights*, *The Subtle Knife* and *The Amber Spyglass*, has been published in more than twenty languages and came second in the recent BBC *Big Read* Top 100 poll. He was made a CBE in 2004.

Contents

Bitter Tears

Funerals and Death-Days 135

Introduction

Life and death!

Is there anything else? It's such a large theme that it must include everything we know, or can ever know – and not only the things we know, but the things we fear, or hope for, or imagine.

It's certainly inspired some of the greatest poets to some of their greatest works. Keats's 'Ode to a Nightingale' is here, as it has to be, and it shows the genius of Keats at its fullest and richest; even when he's wondering about death, and almost giving in to the intoxicating temptation 'To cease upon the midnight with no pain', his talent, his passionate engagement with the sound and the texture of words, can't help celebrating the sensations of life:

> The coming musk-rose, full of dewy wine,
> The murmurous haunt of flies on summer eves.

The grandeur of this theme brings out the best in lesser writers, too. There are not many performances these days of the plays of James Shirley; hardly anything of his is still read except the superb poem 'The glories of our blood and state'. I was very glad to see it in this anthology, because I came across it when I was in my teens, and admired it at once, and learned it by heart. Why did I admire it? Because of its shape, I think. Because of the neatness of the concluding couplet of each stanza:

> Only the actions of the just
> Smell sweet, and blossom in their dust –

1

And because of the grim truthfulness of the whole thing.

Another poem I rejoiced in when I was young (because it made me feel proud and strong and fearless and resolute, none of which things I was in the least) was W. E. Henley's 'Invictus'. I would stride about haughtily, or sit on my own trying to look mysterious and melancholy, telling myself that I was the master of my fate, I was the captain of my soul. Perhaps I was, but it's more likely that I was merely feeling sorry for myself, and that I looked as if I was suffering from indigestion. Never mind! The poem had given me something – a way of thinking and feeling – that I would never have known otherwise. How odd to think that the author of this poem was the real-life model for Robert Louis Stevenson's Long John Silver in *Treasure Island*.

There are some poems here that we know best through the parodies that other writers have based on them. 'You are old, Father William' is one that I only knew through Lewis Carroll's mockery of it in *Alice's Adventures in Wonderland*. It's good to have Southey's original here, though the parody isn't bad, either … And has there ever been a more familiar first line than 'The boy stood on the burning deck?' What we don't know nearly so well is the rest of the poem, but it's a good story.

'The only end of writing', Samuel Johnson said, 'is to enable the readers better to enjoy life or better to endure it'. Consolation is certainly one of the functions of poetry, and the poems in this anthology certainly bear that out. 'In the midst of life, we are in death', as the burial service says in the *Book of Common Prayer*. But even in the presence of death, poetry can console, and distract, and delight. This great theme has produced some of the greatest poetry we have in the language.

Philip Pullman, *July 2004*

Glorious Life

The Windhover
To Christ Our Lord

I caught this morning morning's minion, kingdom of daylight's
     dauphin, dapple-dawn-drawn Falcon, in his riding
  Of the rolling level underneath him steady air, and striding
High there, how he rung upon the rein of a wimpling wing
In his ecstasy! then off, off forth on swing,
  As a skate's heel sweeps smooth on a bow-bend: the hurl
    and gliding
  Rebuffed the big wind. My heart in hiding
Stirred for a bird, – the achieve of, the mastery of the thing!

Brute beauty and valour and act, oh, air, pride, plume here
  Buckle! *and* the fire that breaks from thee then, a billion
Times told lovelier, more dangerous, O my chevalier!

  No wonder of it: shéer plód makes plough down sillion
Shine, and blue-bleak embers, ah my dear,
  Fall, gall themselves, and gash gold-vermilion.

Gerard Manley Hopkins (1844–89)

Ode

We are the music-makers,
    And we are the dreamers of dreams,
Wandering by lone sea-breakers,
    And sitting by desolate streams; –
World-losers and world-forsakers,
    On whom the pale moon gleams:
Yet we are the movers and shakers
    Of the world for ever, it seems.

With wonderful deathless ditties
We build up the world's great cities,
    And out of a fabulous story
    We fashion an empire's glory:
One man with a dream, at pleasure,
    Shall go forth and conquer a crown;
And three with a new song's measure
    Can trample a kingdom down.

We, in the ages lying,
    In the buried past of the earth,
Built Nineveh with our sighing,
    And Babel itself in our mirth;
And o'erthrew them with prophesying
    To the old of the new world's worth;
For each age is a dream that is dying,
    Or one that is coming to birth.

A breath of our inspiration
Is the life of each generation;

A wondrous thing of our dreaming
   Unearthly, impossible seeming –
The soldier, the king, and the peasant
   Are working together in one,
Till our dream shall become their present,
   And their work in the world be done.

They had no vision amazing
Of the goodly house they are raising;
   They had no divine foreshowing
   Of the land to which they are going:
But on one man's soul it hath broken,
   A light that doth not depart;
And his look, or a word he hath spoken,
   Wrought flame in another man's heart.

And therefore today is thrilling
With a past day's late fulfilling;
   And the multitudes are enlisted
   In the faith that their fathers resisted,
And, scorning the dream of tomorrow,
   Are bringing to pass, as they may,
In the world, for its joy or its sorrow,
   The dream that was scorned yesterday.

But we, with our dreaming and singing,
   Ceaseless and sorrowless we!
The glory about us clinging
   Of the glorious futures we see,
Our souls with high music ringing:
   O men! it must ever be

That we dwell, in our dreaming and singing,
    A little apart from ye.

For we are afar with the dawning
    And the suns that are not yet high,
And out of the infinite morning
    Intrepid you hear us cry –
How, spite of your human scorning,
    Once more God's future draws nigh,
And already goes forth the warning
    That ye of the past must die.

Great hail! we cry to the comers
    From the dazzling unknown shore;
Bring us hither your sun and your summers,
    And renew our world as of yore;
You shall teach us your song's new numbers,
    And things that we dreamed not before:
Yea, in spite of a dreamer who slumbers,
    And a singer who sings no more.

                        Arthur O'Shaughnessy (1844–81)

Verses Supposed to Be Written by Alexander Selkirk

I am monarch of all I survey;
My right there is none to dispute;
From the centre all round to the sea
I am lord of the fowl and the brute.
O Solitude! where are the charms
That sages have seen in thy face?
Better dwell in the midst of alarms
Than reign in this horrible place.

I am out of humanity's reach,
I must finish my journey alone,
Never hear the sweet music of speech;
I start at the sound of my own.
The beasts that roam over the plain
My form with indifference see;
They are so unacquainted with man,
Their tameness is shocking to me.

Society, Friendship, and Love
Divinely bestowed upon man,
Oh, had I the wings of a dove
How soon would I taste you again!
My sorrows I then might assuage
In the ways of religion and truth,
Might learn from the wisdom of age,
And be cheered by the sallies of youth.

Religion! what treasure untold
Resides in that heavenly word!
More precious than silver and gold,
Or all that this earth can afford.
But the sound of the church-going bell
These valleys and rocks never heard,
Never sighed at the sound of a knell,
Or smiled when a sabbath appeared.

Ye winds, that have made me your sport,
Convey to this desolate shore
Some cordial endearing report
Of a land I shall visit no more:
My friends, do they now and then send
A wish or a thought after me?
O tell me I yet have a friend,
Though a friend I am never to see.

How fleet is a glance of the mind!
Compared with the speed of its flight,
The tempest itself lags behind,
And the swift-winged arrows of light.
When I think of my own native land
In a moment I seem to be there;
But alas! recollection at hand
Soon hurries me back to despair.

But the seafowl is gone to her nest,
The beast is laid down in his lair;
Even here is a season of rest,
And I to my cabin repair.

There is mercy in every place;
And mercy, encouraging thought!
Gives even affliction a grace
And reconciles man to his lot.

William Cowper (1731–1800)

The Call

Sound, sound the clarion, fill the fife!
  Throughout the sensual world proclaim,
One crowded hour of glorious life
  Is worth an age without a name.

Thomas Osbert Mordaunt (1730–1809)

My Heart Leaps Up

My heart leaps up when I behold
   A rainbow in the sky:
So was it when my life began,
So is it now I am a man,
So be it when I shall grow old
   Or let me die!
The Child is father of the Man:
And I could wish my days to be
Bound each to each by natural piety.

William Wordsworth (1770–1850)

A Birthday

My heart is like a singing bird
   Whose nest is in a watered shoot;
My heart is like an apple-tree
   Whose boughs are bent with thickset fruit;
My heart is like a rainbow shell
   That paddles in a halcyon sea;
My heart is gladder than all these
   Because my love has come to me.

Raise me a dais of silk and down;
   Hang it with vair and purple dyes;
Carve it in doves, and pomegranates,
   And peacocks with a hundred eyes;
Work it in gold and silver grapes,
   In leaves, and silver fleurs-de-lys;
Because the birthday of my life
   Is come, my love is come to me.

Christina Rossetti (1830–94)

Going Down Hill on a Bicycle
A Boy's Song

With lifted feet, hands still,
I am poised, and down the hill
Dart, with heedful mind;
The air goes by in a wind.

Swifter and yet more swift,
Till the heart with a mighty lift
Makes the lungs laugh, the throat cry: –
'O bird, see; see, bird, I fly.

'Is this, is this your joy?
O bird, then I, though a boy,
For a golden moment share
Your feathery life in air!'

Say, heart, is there aught like this
In a world that is full of bliss?
'Tis more than skating, bound
Steel-shod to the level ground.

Speed slackens now, I float
Awhile in my airy boat;
Till, when the wheels scarce crawl,
My feet to the treadles fall.

Alas, that the longest hill
Must end in a vale; but still,
Who climbs with toil, wheresoe'er,
Shall find wings waiting there.

Henry Charles Beeching (1859–1919)

The Song of the Ungirt Runners

We swing ungirded hips,
And lightened are our eyes,
The rain is on our lips,
We do not run for prize.
We know not whom we trust
Nor witherward we fare,
But we run because we must
  Through the great wide air.

The waters of the seas
Are troubled as by storm.
The tempest strips the trees
And does not leave them warm.
Does the tearing tempest pause?
Do the tree-tops ask it why?
So we run without a cause
  'Neath the big bare sky.

The rain is on our lips,
We do not run for prize.
But the storm the water whips
And the wave howls to the skies.
The winds arise and strike it
And scatter it like sand,
And we run because we like it
  Through the broad bright land.

Charles Hamilton Sorley (1895–1915)

On First Looking into Chapman's Homer

Much have I travelled in the realms of gold,
    And many goodly states and kingdoms seen;
    Round many western islands have I been
Which bards in fealty to Apollo hold.
Oft of one wide expanse had I been told
    That deep-browed Homer ruled as his demesne:
    Yet did I never breathe its pure serene
Till I heard Chapman speak out loud and bold:
Then I felt like some watcher of the skies
    When a new planet swims into his ken;
Or like stout Cortez, when with eagle eyes
    He stared at the Pacific – and all his men
Looked at each other with a wild surmise –
    Silent, upon a peak in Darien.

John Keats (1795–1821)

Upon Westminster Bridge
Sept. 3, 1802

Earth has not anything to show more fair:
   Dull would he be of soul who could pass by
A sight so touching in its majesty:
This City now doth, like a garment, wear
The beauty of the morning; silent, bare,
   Ships, towers, domes, theatres, and temples lie
Open unto the fields, and to the sky,
All bright and glittering in the smokeless air.
Never did sun more beautifully steep
   In his first splendour, valley, rock, or hill;
Never saw I, never felt, a calm so deep!
   The river glideth at his own sweet will:
Dear God! the very houses seem asleep;
   And all that mighty heart is lying still!

William Wordsworth (1770–1850)

We Are Transmitters

As we live, we are transmitters of life.
And when we fail to transmit life, life fails to flow through us.

That is part of the mystery of sex, it is a flow onwards.
Sexless people transmit nothing.

And if, as we work, we can transmit life into our work,
life, still more life, rushes into us to compensate, to be ready
and we ripple with life through the days.

Even if it is a woman making an apple dumpling, or a man a stool,
if life goes into the pudding, good is the pudding
good is the stool,
content is the woman, with fresh life rippling in to her,
content is the man.

Give, and it shall be given unto you
is still the truth about life.
But giving life is not so easy.
It doesn't mean handing it out to some mean fool, or letting the living
    dead eat you up.
It means kindling the life-quality where it was not,
even if it's only in the whiteness of a washed pocket-handkerchief.

D.H. Lawrence (1885–1930)

The Glory

The glory of the beauty of the morning, –
The cuckoo crying over the untouched dew;
The blackbird that has found it, and the dove
That tempts me on to something sweeter than love;
White clouds ranged even and fair as new-mown hay;
The heat, the stir, the sublime vacancy
Of sky and meadow and forest and my own heart: –
The glory invites me, yet it leaves me scorning
All I can ever do, all I can be,
Beside the lovely of motion, shape, and hue,
The happiness I fancy fit to dwell
In beauty's presence. Shall I now this day
Begin to seek as far as heaven, as hell,
Wisdom or strength to match this beauty, start
And tread the pale dust pitted with small dark drops,
In hope to find whatever it is I seek,
Hearkening to short-lived happy-seeming things
That we know naught of, in the hazel copse?
Or must I be content with discontent
As larks and swallows are perhaps with wings?
And shall I ask at the day's end once more
What beauty is, and what I can have meant
By happiness? And shall I let all go,
Glad, weary, or both? Or shall I perhaps know
That I was happy oft and oft before,
Awhile forgetting how I am fast pent,
How dreary-swift, with naught to travel to,
Is Time? I cannot bite the day to the core.

Edward Thomas (1878–1917)

The Shepherd Boy Sings in the Valley of Humiliation

He that is down needs fear no fall,
    He that is low, no pride;
He that is humble ever shall
    Have God to be his guide.

I am content with what I have,
    Little be it or much:
And, Lord, contentment still I crave,
    Because Thou savest such.

Fullness to such a burden is
    That go on pilgrimage:
Here little, and hereafter bliss,
    Is best from age to age.

John Bunyan (1628–88)

The World Was All Before Them

In either hand the hastening angel caught
Our lingering parents, and to the eastern gate
Led them direct, and down the cliff as fast
To the subjected plain; then disappeared.
They looking back, all the eastern side beheld
Of Paradise, so late their happy seat,
Waved over by that flaming brand, the gate
With dreadful faces thronged and fiery arms:
Some natural tears they dropped, but wiped them soon;
The world was all before them, where to choose
Their place of rest, and providence their guide:
They hand in hand with wandering steps and slow,
Through Eden took their solitary way.

Paradise Lost, Book XII
John Milton (1608–74)

Think Thou
and Act

Ye Wearie Wayfarer

Question not, but live and labour
   Till yon goal be won,
Helping every feeble neighbour,
   Seeking help from none;
Life is mostly froth and bubble,
   Two things stand like stone,
Kindness in another's trouble,
   Courage in your own.

Adam Lindsay Gordon (1833–70)

On His Blindness

When I consider how my light is spent
Ere half my days, in this dark world and wide,
And that one talent which is death to hide
Lodged with me useless, though my soul more bent

To serve therewith my Maker, and present
My true account, lest He returning chide, –
Doth God exact day-labour, light denied?
I fondly ask: – But Patience, to prevent

That murmur, soon replies; God doth not need
Either man's work or His own gifts: who best
Bear His mild yoke, they serve Him best: His state

Is kingly; thousands at His bidding speed
And post over land and ocean without rest: –
They also serve who only stand and wait.

John Milton (1608–74)

The Character of a Happy Life

How happy is he born and taught
That serveth not another's will;
Whose armour is his honest thought,
And simple truth his utmost skill!

Whose passions not his masters are;
Whose soul is still prepared for death,
Untied unto the world by care
Of public fame or private breath;

Who envies none that chance doth raise,
Nor vice; who never understood
How deepest wounds are given by praise;
Nor rules of state, but rules of good;

Who hath his life from rumours freed;
Whose conscience is his strong retreat;
Whose state can neither flatterers feed,
Nor ruin make oppressors great;

Who God doth late and early pray
More of His grace than gifts to lend;
And entertains the harmless day
With a religious book or friend;

– This man is freed from servile bands
Of hope to rise or fear to fall:
Lord of himself, though not of lands,
And having nothing, yet hath all.

Sir Henry Wotton (1568–1639)

The Village Blacksmith

Under a spreading chestnut tree
  The village smithy stands;
The smith, a mighty man is he,
  With large and sinewy hands;
And the muscles of his brawny arms
  Are strong as iron bands.

His hair is crisp, and black, and long,
  His face is like the tan;
His brow is wet with honest sweat,
  He earns whate'er he can,
And looks the whole world in the face,
  For he owes not any man.

Week in, week out, from morn till night,
  You can hear his bellows blow;
You can hear him swing his heavy sledge,
  With measured beat and slow,
Like a sexton ringing the village bell,
  When the evening sun is low.

And children coming home from school
  Look in at the open door;
They love to see the flaming forge,
  And hear the bellows roar,
And catch the burning sparks that fly
  Like chaff from a threshing floor.

He goes on Sunday to the church,
   And sits among his boys;
He hears the parson pray and preach,
   He hears his daughter's voice,
Singing in the village choir,
   And it makes his heart rejoice.

It sounds to him like her mother's voice,
   Singing in Paradise!
He needs must think of her once more,
   How in the grave she lies;
And with his hard, rough hand he wipes
   A tear out of his eyes.

Toiling, – rejoicing, – sorrowing,
   Onward through life he goes;
Each morning sees some task begin,
   Each evening sees it close;
Something attempted, something done,
   Has earned a night's repose.

Thanks, thanks to thee, my worthy friend,
   For the lesson thou hast taught!
Thus at the flaming forge of life
   Our fortunes must be wrought;
Thus on its sounding anvil shaped
   Each burning deed and thought!

Henry Wadsworth Longfellow (1807–82)

Invictus

Out of the night that covers me,
  Black as the pit from pole to pole,
I thank whatever gods may be
  For my unconquerable soul.

In the fell clutch of circumstance
  I have not winced nor cried aloud,
Under the bludgeonings of chance
  My head is bloody, but unbowed.

Beyond this place of wrath and tears
  Looms but the horror of the shade,
And yet the menace of the years
  Finds and shall find me unafraid.

It matters not how strait the gate,
  How charged with punishments the scroll,
I am the master of my fate:
  I am the captain of my soul.

William Ernest Henley (1849–1903)

The Quiet Life

Climb at Court for me that will
Tottering favour's pinnacle;
All I seek is to lie still.
Settled in some secret nest
In calm leisure let me rest,
And far off the public stage
Pass away my silent age.
Thus when without noise, unknown,
I have lived out all my span,
I shall die, without a groan,
An old honest country man.
Who exposed to others' eyes,
Into his own heart ne'er pries,
Death to him's a strange surprise.

Thyestes
Seneca (*c.* 4 BC–AD 65)
Translated by Andrew Marvell (1621–78)

The Harp Æolian
Letter to J.H. Reynolds, 19 February 1818

My dear Reynolds – I had an idea that a Man might pass a very pleasant life in this manner – Let him on a certain day read a certain page of full Poesy or distilled Prose, and let him wander with it, and muse upon it, and reflect from it, and bring home to it, and prophesy upon it, and dream upon it: until it becomes stale – But when will it do so? Never – When Man has arrived at a certain ripeness in intellect any one grand and spiritual passage serves him as a starting-post towards all 'the two-and-thirty Palaces.' How happy is such a voyage of conception, what delicious diligent indolence! A doze upon a sofa does not hinder it, and a nap upon clover engenders ethereal finger-pointings – the prattle of a child gives it wings, and the converse of middle-age a strength to beat them – a strain of music conducts to 'an odd angle of the Isle,' and when the leaves whisper it puts a girdle round the earth. – Nor will this sparing touch of noble books be any irreverence to their writers – for perhaps the honors paid by Man to Man are trifles in comparison to the benefit done by great works to the 'spirit and pulse of good' by their mere passive existence. Memory should not be called knowledge – Many have original minds who do not think it – they are led away by custom. Now it appears to me that almost any Man may like the spider spin from his own inwards his own airy Citadel – the points of leaves and twigs on which the spider begins her work are few, and she fills the air with a beautiful circuiting. Man should be content with as few points to tip with the fine web of his soul, and weave a tapestry empyrean –

full of symbols for his spiritual eye, of softness for his spiritual touch, of space for his wandering, of distinctness for his luxury. But the minds of mortals are so different and bent on such diverse journeys that it may at first appear impossible for any common taste and fellowship to exist between two or three under these suppositions. It is however quite the contrary. Minds would leave each other in contrary directions, traverse each other in numberless points, and at last greet each other at the journey's end. An old man and a child would talk together and the old man be led on his path and the child left thinking. Man should not dispute or assert, but whisper results to his neighbour, and thus by every germ of spirit sucking the sap from mould ethereal every human might become great, and humanity instead of being a wide heath of furze and briars with here and there a remote oak or pine, would become a grand democracy of forest trees ... Now it is more noble to sit like Jove than to fly like Mercury: – let us not therefore go hurrying about and collecting honey, bee-like, buzzing here and there impatiently from a knowledge of what is to be arrived at. But let us open our leaves like a flower, and be passive and receptive; budding patiently under the eye of Apollo and taking hints from every noble insect that favours us with a visit – Sap will be given us for meat, and dew for drink. I was led into these thoughts, my dear Reynolds, by the beauty of the morning operating on a sense of idleness. I have not read any books – the Morning said I was right – I had no idea but of the Morning, and the Thrush said I was right.

John Keats (1795–1821)

The Vale of Human Life

The first range of hills, that encircles the scanty vale of human life, is the horizon for the majority of its inhabitants. On *its* ridges the common sun is born and departs. From *them* the stars rise, and touching *them* they vanish. By the many, even this range, the natural limit and bulwark of the vale, is but imperfectly known. Its higher ascents are too often hidden by mists and clouds from uncultivated swamps, which few have courage or curiosity to penetrate. To the multitude below these vapours appear, now as the dark haunts of terrific agents, on which none may intrude with impunity; and now all *a-glow*, with colours not their own, they are gazed at as the splendid palaces of happiness and power. But in all ages there have been a few who, measuring and sounding the rivers of the vale at the feet of their furthest inaccessible falls, have learned that the sources must be far higher and far inward; a few, who even in the level streams have detected elements, which neither the vale itself nor the surrounding mountains contained or could supply. How and whence to these thoughts, these strong probabilities, the ascertaining vision, the intuitive knowledge may finally supervene, can be learnt only by the fact. I might oppose to the question the words with which Plotinus supposes Nature to answer a similar difficulty. 'Should any one interrogate her, how she works, if graciously she vouchsafe to listen and speak, she will reply, it behoves thee not to disquiet me with interrogatories, but to understand in silence, even as I am silent, and work without words.'

Biographia Literaria, Chapter XII
Samuel Taylor Coleridge (1772–1834)

The Means to Attain Happy Life

Martial, the things that do attain
   The happy life be these, I find:
The richesse left, not got with pain;
   The fruitful ground, the quiet mind;

The equal friend; no grudge, no strife;
   No charge of rule, nor governance;
Without disease, the healthful life;
   The household of continuance;

The mean diet, no delicate fare;
   True wisdom joined with simpleness;
The night dischargèd of all care,
   Where wine the wit may not oppress.

The faithful wife, without debate;
   Such sleeps as may beguile the night:
Contented with thine own estate
   Ne wish for death, ne fear his might.

Henry Howard, Earl of Surrey (1517–47)

Living In the Present

Above all, we cannot afford not to live in the present. He is blessed over all mortals who loses no moment of the passing life in remembering the past. Unless our philosophy hears the cock crow in every barn-yard within our horizon, it is belated. That sound commonly reminds us that we are growing rusty and antique in our employments and habits of thought. His philosophy comes down to a more recent time than ours. There is something suggested by it that is a newer testament – the gospel according to this moment. He has not fallen astern; he has got up early, and kept up early, and to be where he is, is to be in season, in the foremost rank of time. It is an expression of the health and soundness of nature, a brag for all the world, – healthiness as of a spring burst forth, a new fountain of the Muses, to celebrate this last instant of time. Where he lives no fugitive slave laws are passed. Who has not betrayed his master many times since last he heard that note?

The merit of this bird's strain is in its freedom from all plaintiveness. The singer can easily move us to tears or to laughter, but where is he who can excite in us a pure morning joy? When, in doleful dumps, breaking the awful stillness of our wooden sidewalk on a Sunday, or, perchance a watcher in the house of mourning, I hear a cockerel crow far or near, I think to myself, 'There is one of us well, at any rate,' – and with a sudden gush return to my senses.

Walking
Henry David Thoreau (1817–62)

The Choice

Think thou and act; tomorrow thou shalt die.
  Outstretched in the sun's warmth upon the shore,
  Thou say'st: 'Man's measured path is all gone o'er:
Up all his years, steeply, with strain and sigh,
Man clomb until he touched the truth; and I,
  Even I, am he whom it was destined for.'
  How should this be? Art thou then so much more
Than they who sowed, that thou shouldst reap thereby?

Nay, come up hither. From this wave-washed mound
  Unto the furthest flood-brim look with me;
Then reach on with thy thought till it be drowned.
  Miles and miles distant though the last line be,
And though thy soul sail leagues and leagues beyond, –
  Still, leagues beyond those leagues, there is more sea.

Dante Gabriel Rossetti (1828–82)

The Seven Ages
of Man

All the World's a Stage

All the world's a stage,
And all the men and women merely players:
They have their exits and their entrances;
And one man in his time plays many parts,
His acts being seven ages. At first the infant,
Mewling and puking in the nurse's arms.
And then the whining schoolboy, with his satchel
And shining morning face, creeping like snail
Unwillingly to school. And then the lover,
Sighing like furnace, with a woeful ballad
Made to his mistress' eyebrow. Then a soldier,
Full of strange oaths and bearded like the pard,
Jealous in honour, sudden and quick in quarrel,
Seeking the bubble reputation
Even in the cannon's mouth. And then the justice,
In fair round belly with good capon lined,
With eyes severe, and beard of formal cut,
Full of wise saws and modern instances;
And so he plays his part. The sixth age shifts
Into the lean and slippered pantaloon,
With spectacles on nose and pouch on side,
His youthful hose, well saved, a world too wide
For his shrunk shank; and his big manly voice,
Turning again toward childish treble, pipes
And whistles in his sound. Last scene of all,
That ends this strange eventful history,
Is second childishness and mere oblivion,
Sans teeth, sans eyes, sans taste, sans everything.

As You Like It, Act 2 Scene 7
William Shakespeare (1564–1616)

The Human Seasons

Four Seasons fill the measure of the year;
   There are four seasons in the mind of man.
He has his lusty Spring, when fancy clear
   Takes in all beauty with an easy span.
He has his Summer, when luxuriously
   Spring's honeyed cud of youthful thought he loves
To ruminate, and by such dreaming nigh
   His nearest unto heaven. Quiet coves
His soul has in its Autumn, when his wings
   He furleth close; contented so to look
On mists in idleness – to let fair things
   Pass by unheeded as a threshold brook.
He has his Winter too of pale misfeature,
Or else he would forego his mortal nature.

John Keats (1795–1821)

A Comparison of the Life of Man

Man's life is well comparèd to a feast,
Furnished with choice of all variety:
To it comes Time; and as a bidden guest
He sits him down, in pomp and majesty:
The threefold age of Man, the waiters be.
    Then with an earthen voider, made of clay,
    Comes Death, and takes the table clean away.

Richard Barnfield (1574–1620)

Crabbed Age and Youth

Crabbed age and youth cannot live together:
Youth is full of pleasure, age is full of care;
Youth like summer morn, age like winter weather;
Youth like summer brave, age like winter bare.
Youth is full of sport, age's breath is short;
    Youth is nimble, age is lame;
Youth is hot and bold, age is weak and cold;
Youth is wild, and age is tame.
Age, I do abhor thee; youth, I do adore thee;
    O! my love, my love is young:
Age, I do defy thee: O! sweet shepherd, hie thee,
    For methinks thou stayest too long.

The Passionate Pilgrim
William Shakespeare (1564–1616)

Infant Joy

'I have no name –
I am but two days old.'
What shall I call thee?
'I happy am,
Joy is my name.'
Sweet joy befall thee!

Pretty joy!
Sweet joy, but two days old –
Sweet joy I call thee.
Thou dost smile,
I sing the while –
Sweet joy befall thee!

William Blake (1757–1827)

A New Life

The yellow and crimson leaves came floating down on the still October air; November followed, bleak and dreary; it was more cheerful when the earth put on her beautiful robe of white, which covered up all the grey naked stems, and loaded the leaves of the hollies and evergreens each with its burden of feathery snow. When Ruth sat down to languor and sadness, Miss Benson trotted upstairs, and rummaged up every article of spare or worn-out clothing, and bringing down a variety of strange materials, she tried to interest Ruth in making them up into garments for the poor. But, though Ruth's fingers flew through the work, she still sighed with thought and remembrance. Miss Benson was at first disappointed, and then she was angry. When she heard the low, long sigh, and saw the dreamy eyes filling with glittering tears, she would say, 'What is the matter, Ruth?' in a half-reproachful tone, for the sight of suffering was painful to her; she had done all in her power to remedy it; and, though she acknowledged a cause beyond her reach for Ruth's deep sorrow, and, in fact, loved and respected her all the more for these manifestations of grief, yet at the time they irritated her. Then Ruth would snatch up the dropped work, and stitch away with drooping eyes, from which the hot tears fell fast; and Miss Benson was then angry with herself, yet not at all inclined to agree with Sally when she asked her mistress 'why she kept 'mithering' the poor lass with asking her for ever what was the matter, as if she did not know well enough.' Some element of harmony was wanting – some little angel of peace, in loving whom all hearts and natures should be drawn together, and their discords hushed.

The earth was still 'hiding her guilty front with innocent snow,' when a little baby was laid by the side of the pale, white mother. It was a boy; beforehand she had wished for a girl, as being less likely to feel the want of a father – as being what a mother, worse than widowed, could most effectually shelter. But now she did not think or remember this. What it was, she would not have exchanged for a wilderness of girls. It was her own, her darling, her individual baby, already, though not an hour old, separate and sole in her heart, strangely filling up its measure with love and peace, and even hope. For here was a new, pure, beautiful, innocent life, which she fondly imagined, in that early passion of maternal love, she could guard from every touch of corrupting sin by ever watchful and most tender care. And *her* mother had thought the same, most probably; and thousands of others think the same, and pray to God to purify and cleanse their souls, that they may be fit guardians for their little children. Oh, how Ruth prayed, even while she was yet too weak to speak; and how she felt the beauty and significance of the words, 'Our Father!'

She was roused from this holy abstraction by the sound of Miss Benson's voice. It was very much as if she had been crying.

'Look, Ruth!' it said softly, 'My brother sends you these. They are the first snowdrops in the garden.' And she put them on the pillow by Ruth; the baby lay on the opposite side.

'Won't you look at him?' said Ruth; 'He is so pretty!'

Ruth
Elizabeth Gaskell (1810–65)

To a Child

O child! O new-born denizen
Of life's great city! On thy head
The glory of the morn is shed,
Like a celestial benison!
Here at the portal thou dost stand,
And with thy little hand
Thou openest the mysterious gate
Into the future's undiscovered land.
I see its valves expand,
As at the touch of Fate!
Into those realms of love and hate,
Into that darkness blank and drear,
By some prophetic feeling taught,
I launch the bold, adventurous thought,
Freighted with hope and fear;
As upon subterranean streams,
In caverns unexplored and dark,
Men sometimes launch a fragile bark,
Laden with flickering fire,
And watch its swift-receding beams,
Until at length they disappear,
And in the distant dark expire.
By what astrology of fear or hope
Dare I to cast thy horoscope!
Like the new moon thy life appears;
A little strip of silver light,
And widening outward into night
The shadowy disk of future years!
And yet upon its outer rim,

A luminous circle, faint and dim,
And scarcely visible to us here,
Rounds and completes the perfect sphere;
A prophecy and intimation,
A pale and feeble adumbration,
Of the great world of light, that lies
Behind all human destinies.

Henry Wadsworth Longfellow (1807–82)

To Miss Charlotte Pulteney
in Her Mother's Arms

Timely blossom, infant fair,
Fondling of a happy pair,
Every morn and every night,
Their solicitous delight,
Sleeping, waking, still at ease,
Pleasing, without skill to please,
Little gossip, blithe and hale,
Tattling many a broken tale,
Singing many a tuneless song,
Lavish of a heedless tongue,
Simple maiden, void of art,
Babbling out the very heart,
Yet abandoned to thy will,
Yet imagining no ill,
Yet too innocent to blush,
Like the linlet in the bush
To the mother-linnet's note
Moduling her slender throat,
Chirping forth thy petty joys,
Wanton in the change of toys,
Like the linnet green, in May
Flitting to each bloomy spray,
Wearied then and glad of rest,
Like the linlet in the nest.
This thy present happy lot;
This, in time will be forgot:
Other pleasures, other cares,

Ever-busy time prepares;
And thou shalt in thy daughter see,
This picture, once, resembled thee.

Ambrose Philips (1674–1749)

Spring and Fall
'To a Young Child'

Márgarét, are you gríeving
Over Goldengrove unleaving?
Leáves, líke the things of man, you
With your fresh thoughts care for, can you?
Ah! ás the heart grows older
It will come to such sights colder
By and by, nor spare a sigh
Though worlds of wanwood leafmeal lie;
And yet you wíll weep and know why.
Now no matter, child, the name:
Sórrow's spríngs áre the same.
Nor mouth had, no nor mind, expressed
What heart heard of, ghost guessed:
It ís the blight man was born for,
It is Margaret you mourn for.

Gerard Manley Hopkins (1844–89)

Piano

Softly, in the dusk, a woman is singing to me;
Taking me back down the vista of years, till I see
A child sitting under the piano, in the boom of the tingling strings
And pressing the small, poised feet of a mother who smiles as she
   sings.

In spite of myself, the insidious mastery of song
Betrays me back, till the heart of me weeps to belong
To the old Sunday evenings at home, with winter outside
And hymns in the cosy parlour, the tinkling piano our guide.

So now it is vain for the singer to burst into clamour
With the great black piano apassionato. The glamour
Of childish days is upon me, my manhood is cast
Down in the flood of remembrance, I weep like a child for the past.

D.H. Lawrence (1885–1930)

The Picture of Little T. C. in a Prospect of Flowers

See with what simplicity
This Nymph begins her golden days!
In the green grass she loves to lie,
And there with her fair aspect tames
The wilder flowers, and gives them names;
But only with the roses plays;
         And them does tell
What colour best becomes them, and what smell.

Who can foretell for what high cause
This Darling of the Gods was born!
Yet this is she whose chaster laws
The wanton Love shall one day fear,
And, under her command severe,
See his bow broke and ensigns torn.
         Happy, who can
Appease this virtuous enemy of Man!

O then let me in time compound,
And parley with those conquering eyes;
Ere they have tried their force to wound,
Ere, with their glancing wheels, they drive
In triumph over hearts that strive,
And them that yield but more despise.
         Let me be laid,
Where I may see thy glories from some shade.

Mean time, whilst every verdant thing
It self does at thy beauty charm,
Reform the errors of the Spring;
Make that the tulips may have share
Of sweetness, seeing they are fair;
And roses of their thorns disarm:
           But most procure
That violets may a longer age endure.

But O young beauty of the woods,
Whom Nature courts with fruits and flowers,
Gather the flowers, but spare the buds;
Lest *Flora* angry at thy crime,
To kill her infants in their prime,
Do quickly make the example yours;
           And ere we see,
Nip in the blossom all our hopes and thee.

                        Andrew Marvell (1621–78)

The Schoolboy

I love to rise in a summer morn,
When the birds sing on every tree;
The distant huntsman winds his horn,
And the skylark sings with me –
O what sweet company!

But to go to school in a summer morn,
O it drives all joy away;
Under a cruel eye outworn,
The little ones spend the day
In sighing and dismay.

Ah then at times I drooping sit
And spend many an anxious hour;
Nor in my book can I take delight,
Nor sit in learning's bower,
Worn through with the dreary shower.

How can the bird that is born for joy
Sit in a cage and sing?
How can a child, when fears annoy,
But droop his tender wing
And forget his youthful spring?

Oh, father and mother, if buds are nipped
And blossoms blown away,
And if the tender plants are stripped
Of their joy in the springing day
By sorrow and care's dismay,

How shall the summer arise in joy
Or the summer fruits appear?
Or how shall we gather what griefs destroy,
Or bless the mellowing year
When the blasts of winter appear?

William Blake (1757–1827)

The Toys

My little Son, who looked from thoughtful eyes
And moved and spoke in quiet grown-up wise,
Having my law the seventh time disobeyed,
I struck him, and dismissed
With hard words and unkissed,
His Mother, who was patient, being dead.
Then, fearing lest his grief should hinder sleep,
I visited his bed,
But found him slumbering deep,
With darkened eyelids, and their lashes yet
From his late sobbing wet.
And I, with moan,
Kissing away his tears, left others of my own;
For, on a table drawn beside his head,
He had put, within his reach,
A box of counters and a red-veined stone,
A piece of glass abraded by the beach
And six or seven shells,
A bottle with bluebells
And two French copper coins, ranged there with careful art,
To comfort his sad heart.
So when that night I prayed
To God, I wept, and said:
Ah, when at last we lie with tranced breath,
Not vexing Thee in death,
And Thou rememberest of what toys
We made our joys,
How weakly understood,
Thy great commanded good,

Then, fatherly not less
Than I whom Thou hast moulded from the clay,
Thou'lt leave Thy wrath, and say,
'I will be sorry for their childishness.'

Coventry Patmore (1823–96)

Sonnet 8

That time of year thou may'st in me behold
When yellow leaves, or none, or few, do hang
Upon those boughs which shake against the cold –
Bare ruined choirs where late the sweet birds sang.
In me thou see'st the twilight of such day
As after sunset fadeth in the west,
Which by and by black night doth take away,
Death's second self, that seals up all in rest.
In me thou see'st the glowing of such fire
That on the ashes of his youth doth lie,
As the death-bed whereon it must expire,
Consumed with that which it was nourished by.
   This thou perceiv'st, which makes thy love more strong
   To love that well which thou must leave ere long.

William Shakespeare (1564–1616)

He Never Expected Much
A Reflection on My Eighty-Sixth Birthday

Well, World, you have kept faith with me,
        Kept faith with me;
Upon the whole you have proved to be
        Much as you said you were.
Since as a child I used to lie
Upon the leaze and watch the sky,
Never, I own, expected I
        That life would all be fair.

'Twas then you said, and since have said,
        Times since have said,
In that mysterious voice you shed
        From clouds and hills around:
'Many have loved me desperately,
Many with smooth serenity,
While some have shown contempt of me
        Till they dropped underground.

'I do not promise overmuch,
        Child; overmuch;
Just neutral-tinted haps and such,'
        You said to minds like mine.
Wise warning for your credit's sake!
Which I for one failed not to take,
And hence could stem such strain and ache
        As each year might assign.

                                Thomas Hardy (1840–1928)

The Old Man's Comforts
and How he Gained Them

'You are old, Father William,' the young man cried,
   'The few locks that are left you are grey;
You are hale, Father William, a hearty old man;
   Now tell me the reason, I pray.'

'In the days of my youth,' Father William replied,
   'I remembered that youth would fly fast,
And abused not my health and my vigour at first,
   That I never might need them at last.'

'You are old, Father William,' the young man cried,
   'And pleasures with youth pass away;
And yet you lament not the days that are gone;
   Now tell me the reason, I pray.'

'In the days of my youth,' Father William replied,
   'I remembered that youth could not last;
I thought of the future; whatever I did,
   That I never might grieve for the past.'

'You are old, Father William,' the young man cried,
   'And life must be hastening away;
You are cheerful, and love to converse upon death;
   Now tell me the reason, I pray.'

'I am cheerful, young man,' Father William replied,
   'Let the cause thy attention engage;
In the days of my youth I remembered my God,
   And He hath not forgotten my age.'

                              Robert Southey (1774–1843)

The Old Familiar Faces

I have had playmates, I have had companions,
In my days of childhood, in my joyful school-days,
All, all are gone, the old familiar faces.

I have been laughing, I have been carousing,
Drinking late, sitting late, with my bosom cronies,
All, all are gone, the old familiar faces.

I loved a love once, fairest among women:
Closed are her doors on me, I must not see her –
All, all are gone, the old familiar faces.

I have a friend, a kinder friend hath no man;
Like an ingrate, I left my friend abruptly;
Left him, to muse on the old familiar faces.

Ghost-like I paced round the haunts of my childhood,
Earth seemed a desert I was bound to traverse,
Seeking to find the old familiar faces.

Friend of my bosom, thou more than a brother,
Why wert not thou born in my father's dwelling?
So might we talk of the old familiar faces –

How some they have died, and some they have left me,
And some are taken from me; all are departed;
All, all are gone, the old familiar faces.

Charles Lamb (1775–1834)

Oft in the Stilly Night

Oft in the stilly night
  Ere Slumber's chain has bound me,
Fond Memory brings the light
Of other days around me;
    The smiles, the tears,
    Of boyhood's years,
  The words of love then spoken,
    The eyes that shone,
    Now dimmed and gone,
  The cheerful hearts now broken!
Thus in the stilly night,
  Ere Slumber's chain has bound me,
Sad Memory brings the light
  Of other days around me.

When I remember all
  The friends so linked together,
I've seen around me fall,
  Like leaves in wintry weather:
    I feel like one
    Who treads alone
  Some banquet-hall deserted,
    Whose lights are fled,
    Whose garland's dead,
  And all but he departed!
Thus in the stilly night,
  Ere Slumber's chain has bound me,
Fond Memory brings the light
  Of other days around me.

Thomas Moore (1779–1852)

Rain

Rain, midnight rain, nothing but the wild rain
On this bleak hut, and solitude, and me
Remembering again that I shall die
And neither hear the rain nor give it thanks
For washing me cleaner than I have been
Since I was born into this solitude.
Blessed are the dead that the rain rains upon:
But here I pray that none whom once I loved
Is dying tonight or lying still awake
Solitary, listening to the rain,
Either in pain or thus in sympathy
Helpless among the living and the dead,
Like a cold water among broken reeds,
Myriads of broken reeds all still and stiff,
Like me who have no love which this wild rain
Has not dissolved except the love of death,
If love it be for what is perfect and
Cannot, the tempest tells me, disappoint.

Edward Thomas (1878–1917)

Ulysses

It little profits that an idle king,
By this still hearth, among these barren crags,
Matched with an aged wife, I mete and dole
Unequal laws unto a savage race,
That hoard, and sleep, and feed, and know not me.
I cannot rest from travel: I will drink
Life to the lees: all times I have enjoyed
Greatly, have suffered greatly, both with those
That loved me, and alone; on shore, and when
Through scudding drifts the rainy Hyades
Vexed the dim sea. I am become a name;
For always roaming with a hungry heart
Much have I seen and known: cities of men
And manners, climates, councils, governments,
Myself not least, but honoured of them all, –
And drunk delight of battle with my peers,
Far on the ringing plains of windy Troy.
I am a part of all that I have met;
Yet all experience is an arch wherethrough
Gleams that untravelled world, whose margin fades
For ever and for ever when I move.
How dull it is to pause, to make an end,
To rust unburnished, not to shine in use!
As though to breathe were life. Life piled on life
Were all too little, and of one to me
Little remains: but every hour is saved
From that eternal silence, something more,
A bringer of new things; and vile it were
For some three suns to store and hoard myself,

And this gray spirit yearning in desire
To follow knowledge, like a sinking star,
Beyond the utmost bound of human thought.

Alfred, Lord Tennyson (1809–92)

What Is Life?

And what is Life? An hourglass on the run
A mist retreating from the morning sun
   A busy bustling still repeated dream
Its length? A moment's pause, a moment's thought
   And happiness? A bubble on the stream
That in the act of seizing shrinks to nought

Vain hopes – what are they? Puffing gales of morn
That of its charms divests the dewy lawn
   And robs each flowret of its gem and dies
A cobweb hiding disappointment's thorn
   Which stings more keenly through the thin disguise

And thou, O trouble? Nothing can suppose,
And sure the Power of Wisdom only knows,
   What need requireth thee.
So free and liberal as thy bounty flows,
   Some necessary cause must surely be.

And what is death? Is still the cause unfound
The dark mysterious name of horrid sound
   A long and lingering sleep the weary crave –
And peace – where can its happiness abound?
   Nowhere at all but Heaven and the grave

Then what is Life? When stripped of its disguise
   A thing to be desired it cannot be
Since every thing that meets our foolish eyes
   Gives proof sufficient of its vanity

'Tis but a trial all must undergo
　　To teach unthankful mortals how to prize
That happiness vain man's denied to know
　　Until he's called to claim it in the skies.

John Clare (1793–1864)

Parting

My life closed twice before its close –
It yet remains to see
If Immortality unveil
A third event to me

So huge, so hopeless to conceive
As these that twice befell.
Parting is all we know of heaven,
And all we need of hell.

Emily Dickinson (1830–86)

Finis

I strove with none, for none was worth my strife:
    Nature I loved and, next to Nature, Art:
I warmed both hands before the fire of Life;
    It sinks; and I am ready to depart.

Walter Savage Landor (1775–1864)

Tomorrow Will Be Dying

They Are Not Long

They are not long, the weeping and the laughter,
    Love and desire and hate:
I think they have no portion in us after
    We pass the gate.

They are not long, the days of wine and roses:
    Out of a misty dream
Our path emerges for a while, then closes
    Within a dream.

Ernest Dowson (1867–1900)

What Is Our Life?

What is our life? a play of passion,
Our mirth the music of division,
Our mother's wombs the tiring houses be,
Where we are dressed for this short comedy,
Heaven the judicious sharp spectator is,
That sits and marks who still doth act amiss,
Our graves that hide us from the searching sun
Are like drawn curtains when the play is done.
Thus march we playing to our latest rest,
Only we die in earnest, that's no jest.

Sir Walter Raleigh (1554–1618)

To The Virgins, to Make Much of Time

Gather ye rosebuds while ye may,
   Old Time is still a-flying:
And this same flower that smiles today
   Tomorrow will be dying.

The glorious lamp of heaven, the sun,
   The higher he's a-getting,
The sooner will his race be run,
   And nearer he's to setting.

That age is best which is the first,
   When youth and blood are warmer;
But being spent, the worse, and worst
   Times still succeed the former.

Then be not coy, but use your time,
   And while ye may, go marry:
For having lost but once your prime,
   You may for ever tarry.

Robert Herrick (1591–1674)

Ode to a Nightingale

My heart aches, and a drowsy numbness pains
   My sense, as though of hemlock I had drunk,
Or emptied some dull opiate to the drains
   One minute past, and Lethe-wards had sunk:
'Tis not through envy of thy happy lot,
   But being too happy in thy happiness, –
      That thou, light-winged Dryad of the trees,
      In some melodious plot
   Of beechen green, and shadows numberless,
      Singest of summer in full-throated ease.

O, for a draught of vintage! that hath been
   Cooled a long age in the deep-delved earth,
Tasting of Flora and the country-green,
   Dance, and Provençal song, and sunburnt mirth.
O for a beaker full of the warm South,
   Full of the true, the blushful Hippocrene,
      With beaded bubbles winking at the brim,
      And purple-stained mouth;
   That I might drink, and leave the world unseen,
      And with thee fade away into the forest dim.

Fade far away, dissolve, and quite forget
   What thou among the leaves hast never known,
The weariness, the fever, and the fret
   Here, where men sit and hear each other groan;
Where palsy shakes a few, sad, last grey hairs,
   Where youth grows pale, and spectre-thin, and dies;
      Where but to think is to be full of sorrow

And leaden-eyed despairs;
　Where Beauty cannot keep her lustrous eyes,
　　Or new Love pine at them beyond tomorrow.

Away! away! for I will fly to thee,
　Not charioted by Bacchus and his pards,
But on the viewless wings of Poesy,
　Though the dull brain perplexes and retards:
Already with thee! tender is the night,
　And haply the Queen-Moon is on her throne,
　　Clustered around by all her starry Fays;
　　But here there is no light
　Save what from heaven is with the breezes blown
　　Through verdurous glooms and winding mossy ways.

I cannot see what flowers are at my feet,
　Nor what soft incense hangs upon the boughs,
But, in embalmed darkness, guess each sweet
　Wherewith the seasonable month endows
The grass, the thicket, and the fruit-tree wild;
　White hawthorn, and the pastoral eglantine;
　　Fast fading violets covered up in leaves;
　　And mid-May's eldest child
　The coming musk-rose, full of dewy wine,
　　The murmurous haunt of flies on summer eves.

Darkling I listen; and for many a time
　I have been half in love with easeful Death,
Called him soft names in many a mused rhyme,
　To take into the air my quiet breath;
Now more than ever seems it rich to die,

To cease upon the midnight with no pain,
   While thou art pouring forth thy soul abroad
   In such an ecstasy!
Still wouldst thou sing, and I have ears in vain –
   To thy high requiem become a sod.

Thou wast not born for death, immortal Bird!
   No hungry generations tread thee down;
The voice I hear this passing night was heard
   In ancient days by emperor and clown:
Perhaps the selfsame song that found a path
   Through the sad heart of Ruth, when, sick for home,
     She stood in tears amid the alien corn;
     The same that oft-times hath
   Charmed magic casements, opening on the foam
     Of perilous seas, in faery lands forlorn.

Forlorn! the very word is like a bell
   To toll me back from thee to my sole self!
Adieu! the fancy cannot cheat so well
   As she is famed to do, deceiving elf.
Adieu! adieu! thy plaintive anthem fades
   Past the near meadows, over the still stream,
     Up the hill-side; and now 'tis buried deep
     In the next valley-glades:
   Was it a vision, or a waking dream?
     Fled is that music: – do I wake or sleep?

John Keats (1795–1821)

Dirge In Woods

A wind sways the pines,
        And below
Not a breath of wild air;
Still as the mosses that glow
On the flooring and over the lines
Of the roots here and there.
The pine-tree drops its dead;
They are quiet, as under the sea.
Overhead, overhead
Rushes life in a race,
As the clouds the clouds chase;
        And we go,
And we drop like the fruits of the tree,
        Even we,
        Even so.

George Meredith (1828–1909)

Vanitas Vanitatum

All the flowers of the spring
Meet to perfume our burying;
These have but their growing prime,
And man does flourish but his time:
Survey our progress from our birth –
We are set, we grow, we turn to earth.
Courts adieu, and all delights,
All bewitching appetites!
Sweetest breath and clearest eye
Like perfumes go out and die;
And consequently this is done
As shadows wait upon the sun.
Vain the ambition of kings
Who seek by trophies and dead things
To leave a living name behind,
And weave but nets to catch the wind.

John Webster (*c.*1578–1626)

Elegy Written in a Country Churchyard

The curfew tolls the knell of parting day,
The lowing herd wind slowly o'er the lea,
The ploughman homeward plods his weary way,
And leaves the world to darkness and to me.

Now fades the glimmering landscape on the sight,
And all the air a solemn stillness holds,
Save where the beetle wheels his droning flight,
And drowsy tinklings lull the distant folds:

Save that from yonder ivy-mantled tower
The moping owl does to the moon complain
Of such as, wandering near her secret bower,
Molest her ancient solitary reign.

Beneath those rugged elms, that yew-tree's shade,
When heaves the turf in many a mouldering heap,
Each in his narrow cell for ever laid,
The rude forefathers of the hamlet sleep.

The breezy call of incense-breathing morn,
The swallow twittering from the straw-built shed,
The cock's shrill clarion, or the echoing horn,
No more shall rouse them from their lowly bed.

For them no more the blazing hearth shall burn
Or busy housewife ply her evening care:
No children run to lisp their sire's return,
Or climb his knees the envied kiss to share.

Oft did the harvest to their sickle yield,
Their furrow oft the stubborn glebe has broke;
How jocund did they drive their team afield!
How bowed the woods beneath their sturdy stroke!

Let not Ambition mock their useful toil,
Their homely joys, and destiny obscure;
Nor Grandeur hear with a disdainful smile
The short and simple annals of the poor.

The boast of heraldry, the pomp of power,
And all that beauty, all that wealth e'er gave,
Awaits alike th'inevitable hour: –
The paths of glory lead but to the grave.

Nor you, ye Proud, impute to these the fault
If Memory o'er their tomb no trophies raise,
Where through the long-drawn aisle and fretted vault
The pealing anthem swells the note of praise.

Can storied urn or animated bust
Back to its mansion call the fleeting breath?
Can Honour's voice provoke the silent dust,
Or Flattery soothe the dull cold ear of Death?

Perhaps in this neglected spot is laid
Some heart once pregnant with celestial fire;
Hands, that the rod of empire might have swayed,
Or waked to ecstasy the living lyre.

But Knowledge to their eyes her ample page
Rich with the spoils of time, did ne'er unroll;
Chill Penury repressed their noble rage,
And froze the genial current of the soul.

Full many a gem of purest ray serene
The dark unfathomed caves of ocean bear:
Full many a flower is born to blush unseen,
And waste its sweetness on the desert air.

Some village-Hampden, that with dauntless breast
The little tyrant of his fields withstood,
Some mute inglorious Milton here may rest,
Some Cromwell, guiltless of his country's blood.

Th'applause of listening senates to command,
The threats of pain and ruin to despise,
To scatter plenty o'er a smiling land,
And read their history in a nation's eyes

Their lot forbade: nor circumscribed alone
Their growing virtues, but their crimes confined;
Forbade to wade through slaughter to a throne,
And shut the gates of mercy on mankind;

The struggling pangs of conscious truth to hide,
To quench the blushes of ingenuous shame,
Or heap the shrine of Luxury and Pride
With incense kindled at the Muse's flame.

Far from the madding crowd's ignoble strife
Their sober wishes never learned to stray;
Along the cool sequestered vale of life
They kept the noiseless tenor of their way.

Yet even these bones from insult to protect
Some frail memorial still erected nigh,
With uncouth rhymes and shapeless sculpture decked,
Implores the passing tribute of a sigh.

Their name, their years, spelt by th'unlettered Muse,
The place of fame and elegy supply:
And many a holy text around she strews,
That teach the rustic moralist to die.

For who, to dumb forgetfulness a prey,
This pleasing anxious being e'er resigned,
Left the warm precincts of the cheerful day,
Nor cast one longing, lingering look behind?

On some fond breast the parting soul relies,
Some pious drops the closing eye requires;
Even from the tomb the voice of Nature cries,
Even in our ashes live their wonted fires.

For thee, who, mindful of th'unhonoured dead,
Dost in these lines their artless tale relate;
If chance, by lonely Contemplation led,
Some kindred spirit shall inquire thy fate, –

Haply some hoary-headed swain may say,
Oft have we seen him at the peep of dawn
Brushing with hasty steps the dews away,
To meet the sun upon the upland lawn;

There at the foot of yonder nodding beech
That wreathes its old fantastic roots so high,
His listless length at noon-tide would he stretch,
And pore upon the brook that babbles by.

Hard by yon wood, now smiling as in scorn,
Muttering his wayward fancies he would rove;
Now drooping, woeful-wan, like one forlorn,
Or crazed with care, or crossed in hopeless love.

One morn I missed him on the customed hill,
Along the heath, and near his favourite tree;
Another came; nor yet beside the rill,
Nor up the lawn, nor at the wood was he;

The next with dirges due in sad array
Slow through the church-way path we saw him borne, –
Approach and read (for thou canst read) the lay
Graved on the stone beneath yon aged thorn.

Thomas Gray (1716–71)

On the Tombs in Westminster Abbey

Mortality, behold and fear!
What a change of flesh is here!
Think how many royal bones
Sleep within this heap of stones:
Here they lie had realms and lands,
Who now want strength to stir their hands:
Where from their pulpits sealed with dust
They preach, 'In greatness is no trust.'
Here's an acre sown indeed
With the richest, royallest seed
That the earth did e'er suck in
Since the first man died for sin:
Here the bones of birth have cried –
'Though gods they were, as men they died.'
Here are sands, ignoble things,
Dropt from the ruined sides of kings;
Here's a world of pomp and state,
Buried in dust, once dead by fate.

Francis Beaumont (1584–1616)

Sic Vita

Like to the falling of a star;
Or as the flights of eagles are;
Or like the fresh spring's gaudy hue;
Or silver drops of morning dew;
Or like a wind that chafes the flood;
Or bubbles which on water stood;
Even such is man, whose borrowed light
Is straight called in, and paid to night.

The wind blows out, the bubble dies;
The spring entombed in autumn lies;
The dew dries up, the star is shot;
The flight is past, and man forgot.

Henry King, Bishop of Chichester (1592–1669)

No Triumph, No Defeat

Such, such is Death: no triumph: no defeat:
Only an empty pail, a slate rubbed clean,
A merciful putting away of what has been.

And this we know: Death is not Life effect,
Life crushed, the broken pail. We who have seen
So marvellous things know well the end not yet.

Victor and vanquished are a-one in death:
Coward and brave: friend, foe. Ghosts do not say
'Come, what was your record when you drew breath?'
But a big blot has hid each yesterday
So poor, so manifestly incomplete.
And your bright promise, withered long and sped,
Is touched, stirs, rises, opens and grows sweet
And blossoms and is you, when you are dead.

Charles Hamilton Sorley (1895–1915)

Death the Leveller

The glories of our blood and state
   Are shadows, not substantial things;
There is no armour against Fate;
   Death lays his icy hand on kings:
      Sceptre and Crown
      Must tumble down,
And in the dust be equal made
With the poor crooked scythe and spade.

Some men with swords may reap the field,
   And plant fresh laurels where they kill:
But their strong nerves at last must yield;
   They tame but one another still:
      Early or late
      They stoop to fate,
And must give up their murmuring breath
When they, pale captives, creep to death.

The garlands wither on your brow;
   Then boast no more your mighty deeds!
Upon Death's purple altar now
   See where the victor-victim bleeds.
      Your heads must come
      To the cold tomb:
Only the actions of the just
Smell sweet and blossom in their dust.

James Shirley (1596–1666)

Madam Life's a Piece in Bloom

Madam Life's a piece in bloom
   Death goes dogging everywhere:
She's the tenant of the room,
   He's the ruffian on the stair.

You shall see her as a friend,
   You shall bilk him once and twice;
But he'll trap you in the end,
   And he'll stick you for her price.

With his kneebones at your chest,
   And his knuckles in your throat,
You would reason – plead – protest!
   Clutching at her petticoat;

But she's heard it all before,
   Well she knows you've had your fun,
Gingerly she gains the door,
   And your little job is done.

William Ernest Henley (1849–1903)

from Lament for the Makers

I that in heill[1] was and gladness
Am troubled now with great sickness
And feebled with infirmity: –
  Timor Mortis conturbat me.[2]

Our plesance here is all vain glory,
This false world is but transitory,
The flesh is bruckle,[3] the fiend is slee:[4] –
  Timor Mortis conturbat me.

The state of man does change and vary,
Now sound, now sick, now blyth, now sary,
Now dansand[5] merry, now like to die: –
  Timor Mortis conturbat me.

No state in Earth here stands sicker;[6]
As with the wind waves the wicker[7]
So wanes this world's vanity: –
  Timor Mortis conturbat me.

William Dunbar (*c.*1456–1513)

[1] health
[2] the fear of death confounds me
[3] brittle, feeble
[4] sly
[5] dancing
[6] sure
[7] willow

Life

Life! I know not what thou art,
But know that thou and I must part;
And when, or how, or where we met,
I own to me's a secret yet.
But this I know, when thou art fled,
Where'er they lay these limbs, this head,
No clod so valueless shall be
As all that then remains of me.

O whither, whither dost thou fly?
Where bend unseen thy trackless course?
   And in this strange divorce,
Ah, tell where I must seek this compound I?
To the vast ocean of empyreal flame
   From whence thy essence came
Dost thou thy flight pursue, when freed
From matter's base encumbering weed?
   Or dost thou, hid from sight,
   Wait, like some spell-bound knight,
Through blank oblivious years th'appointed hour
To break thy trance and reassume thy power?
Yet canst thou without thought or feeling be?
O say, what art thou, when no more thou'rt thee?

Life! we have been long together,
Through pleasant and through cloudy weather;
   'Tis hard to part when friends are dear;
   Perhaps 'twill cost a sigh, a tear; –

Then steal away, give little warning,
    Choose thine own time;
Say not Good-night, but in some brighter clime
    Bid me Good-morning!

Anna Laetitia Barbauld (1743–1825)

Upon the Image of Death

Before my face the picture hangs,
That daily should put me in mind
Of those cold qualms and bitter pangs,
That shortly I am like to find:
   But yet, alas, full little I
   Do think hereon that I must die.

I often look upon a face
Most ugly, grisly, bare, and thin;
I often view the hollow place,
Where eyes and nose had sometimes been;
   I see the bones across that lie,
   Yet little think that I must die.

I read the label underneath,
That telleth me whereto I must;
I see the sentence eke that sayeth
'Remember, man, that thou art dust!'
   But yet, alas, but seldom I
   Do think indeed that I must die.

Continually at my bed's head
A hearse doth hang, which doth me tell,
That I ere morning may be dead,
Though now I feel myself full well:
   But yet, alas, for all this, I
   Have little mind that I must die.

The gown which I do use to wear,
The knife wherewith I cut my meat,
And eke that old and ancient chair

Which is my only usual seat;
   All those do tell me I must die,
   And yet my life amend not I.

My ancestors are turned to clay,
And many of my mates are gone;
My youngers daily drop away,
And can I think to 'scape alone?
   No, no, I know that I must die,
   And yet my life amend not I.

Not Solomon for all his wit,
Nor Samson, though he were so strong,
No king nor person ever yet
Could 'scape, but death laid him along:
   Wherefore I know that I must die,
   And yet my life amend not I.

Though all the East did quake to hear
Of Alexander's dreadful name,
And all the West did likewise fear
To hear of Julius Caesar's fame,
   Yet both by death in dust now lie.
   Who then can 'scape, but he must die?

If none can 'scape death's dreadful dart,
If rich and poor his beck obey,
If strong, if wise, if all do smart,
Then I to 'scape shall have no way.
   Oh, grant me grace, Oh God, that I
   My life may mend sith I must die.

Robert Southwell (1561–95)

A Ballad of Past Meridian

Last night returning from my twilight walk
I met the grey mist Death, whose eyeless brow
Was bent on me, and from his hand of chalk
He reached me flowers as from a withered bough:
O Death, what bitter nosegays givest thou!

Death said, 'I gather', and pursued his way.
Another stood by me, a shape in stone,
Sword-hacked and iron-stained, with breasts of clay,
And metal veins that sometimes fiery shone:
O Life, how naked and how hard when known!

Life said, 'As thou hast carved me, such am I.'
Then Memory, like the nightjar on the pine,
And sightless hope, a woodlark in night sky,
Joined notes of Death and Life till night's decline:
Of Death, of Life, those inwound notes are mine.

George Meredith (1828–1909)

When I Have Fears That I May Cease to Be

When I have fears that I may cease to be
  Before my pen has gleaned my teeming brain,
Before high-piled books, in charactery,
  Hold like rich garners the full-ripened grain;
When I behold, upon the night's starred face,
  Huge cloudy symbols of a high romance,
And think that I may never live to trace
  Their shadows, with the magic hand of chance;
And when I feel, fair creature of an hour!
  That I shall never look upon thee more,
Never have relish in the faery power
  Of unreflecting love! – then on the shore
Of the wide world I stand alone, and think
Till love and fame to nothingness do sink.

John Keats (1795–1821)

Dover Beach

The sea is calm tonight.
The tide is full, the moon lies fair
Upon the straits; – on the French coast, the light
Gleams, and is gone; the cliffs of England stand,
Glimmering and vast, out in the tranquil bay.
Come to the window, sweet is the night air!
Only, from the long line of spray
Where the sea meets the moon-blanched sand,
Listen! you hear the grating roar
Of pebbles which the waves draw back, and fling,
At their return, up the high strand,
Begin, and cease, and then again begin,
With tremulous cadence slow, and bring
The eternal note of sadness in.

Sophocles long ago
Heard it on the Ægean, and it brought
Into his mind the turbid ebb and flow
Of human misery; we
Find also in the sound a thought,
Hearing it by this distant northern sea.

The Sea of Faith
Was once, too, at the full, and round earth's shore
Lay like the folds of a bright girdle furled.
But now I only hear
Its melancholy, long, withdrawing roar,
Retreating, to the breath
Of the night-wind, down the vast edges drear
And naked shingles of the world.

Ah, love, let us be true
To one another! for the world, which seems
To lie before us like a land of dreams,
So various, so beautiful, so new,
Hath really neither joy, nor love, nor light,
Nor certitude, nor peace, nor help for pain;
And we are here as on a darkling plain
Swept with confused alarms of struggle and flight,
Where ignorant armies clash by night.

Matthew Arnold (1822–88)

A Time for Everything

To every thing there is a season, and a time to every purpose
    under the heaven:
a time to be born, and a time to die; a time to plant, and a time
    to pluck up that which is planted;
a time to kill, and a time to heal; a time to break down, and a
    time to build up;
a time to weep, and a time to laugh; a time to mourn, and a
    time to dance;
a time to cast away stones, and a time to gather stones together,
    a time to embrace, and a time to refrain from embracing;
a time to get, and a time to lose; a time to keep, and a time to
    cast away;
a time to rend, and a time to sew; a time to keep silence, and a
    time to speak;
a time to love, and a time to hate; a time of war, and a time of
    peace.

The Bible, Ecclesiastes 3
The King James Version (1611)

Bitter Tears

Heraclitus

They told me, Heraclitus, they told me you were dead;
They brought me bitter news to hear and bitter tears to shed.
I wept as I remembered how often you and I
Had tired the sun with talking and sent him down the sky.

And now that thou art lying, my dear old Carian guest,
A handful of gray ashes, long, long ago at rest,
Still are thy pleasant voices, thy nightingales, awake,
For Death, he taketh all away, but them he cannot take.

Callimachus (*c.* 310–246 BC)
Translated by William Cory (1823–92)

On His Brother's Death

By ways remote and distant waters sped,
Brother, to thy sad graveside am I come,
That I may give the last gifts to the dead,
And vainly parley with thine ashes dumb:
Since she who now bestows and now denies
Hath taken thee, hapless brother, from mine eyes.
But lo! these gifts, the heirlooms of past years,
Are made sad things to grace thy coffin shell;
Take them, all drenched with a brother's tears,
And, brother, for all time, hail and farewell!

Catullus (87–54 BC)
Translated by Aubrey Beardsley (1872–98)

Early Death

She passed away like morning dew
   Before the sun was high;
So brief her time, she scarcely knew
   The meaning of a sigh.

As round the rose its soft perfume,
   Sweet love around her floated;
Admired she grew – while mortal doom
   Crept on, unfeared, unnoted.

Love was her guardian Angel here,
   But Love to Death resigned her;
Though Love was kind, why should we fear
   But holy Death is kinder?

Hartley Coleridge (1796–1849)

Requiescat

Strew on her roses, roses,
    And never a spray of yew.
In quiet she reposes:
    Ah! would that I did too.

Her mirth the world required:
    She bathed it in smiles of glee.
But her heart was tired, tired,
    And now they let her be.

Her life was turning, turning,
    In mazes of heat and sound.
But for peace her soul was yearning,
    And now peace laps her round.

Her cabined, ample Spirit,
    It fluttered and failed for breath.
Tonight it doth inherit
    The vasty hall of Death.

Matthew Arnold (1822–88)

The Gargoyle

Here now stood the tomb as the men had stated, snow-white and shapely in the gloom, with a head and foot stone, an enclosing border of marblework uniting them. In the midst was mould, suitable for plants.

Troy deposited his basket beside the tomb, and vanished for a few minutes. When he returned he carried a spade and a lantern, the light of which he directed for a few moments upon the tomb, whilst he read the inscription. He hung his lantern on the lowest bough of the yew tree, and took from his basket flower-roots of several varieties. There were bundles of snowdrop, hyacinth and crocus bulbs, violets and double daisies, which were to bloom in early spring, and of carnations, pinks, picotees, lilies of the valley, heartsease, forget-me-not, summer's farewell and others, for the later seasons of the year.

Troy laid these out upon the grass, and with an impassive face set to work to plant them. The snowdrops were arranged in a row on the outside of the coping, the remainder within the enclosure of the grave. The crocuses and hyacinths were to grow in rows: some of the summer flowers he placed over her head and feet; the lilies and forget-me-nots over her heart. The remainder were dispersed in the spaces between these.

Troy, in his prostration at this time, had no perception that in the futility of these romantic doings, dictated by a remorseful reaction from previous indifference, there was any element of absurdity. Deriving his idiosyncrasies from both sides of the Channel, he showed at such junctures as the present the inelasticity of the Englishman, and the

111

blindness to the line where sentiment verges on mawkish-ness so characteristic of the French.

It was a cloudy, muggy, and very dark night, and the rays from Troy's lantern spread into the two old yews with a strange illuminating power, flickering, as it seemed, up to the black ceiling of cloud above. He felt a large drop of rain upon the back of his hand; and presently one came and entered the open side of the lantern, whereupon the candle sputtered and went out. Troy was weary, and it being now not far from midnight, and the rain threatening to increase, he resolved to leave the finishing touches of his labour until the day should break. He groped along the wall and over the graves in the dark till he found himself round at the south side. Here he entered the porch, and reclining upon the bench within, fell asleep.

The tower of Weatherbury Church was a square erec-tion of fourteenth-century date, having two stone gargoyles on each of the four faces of its parapet. Of these eight carved protuberances only two at this date continued to serve the purpose of their erection – that of spouting the water from the lead roof within. One mouth in each front had been closed by bygone churchwardens as superfluous, and two others were broken away and choked – a matter not of much consequence to the well-being of the tower, for the two mouths which still remained open and active were gaping enough to do all the work.

It has been sometimes argued that there is no truer criterion of the vitality of any given art-period than the power of the master-spirits of that time in grotesque; and certainly in the instance of Gothic art there is no disputing the proposition. Weatherbury tower was a somewhat early instance of the use of an ornamental parapet in parish as distinct from cathedral churches, and the gargoyles, which are the necessary correlatives of a parapet, were exceptionally prominent – of the boldest cut that the hand could shape, and of the most original design that a human brain could conceive. There was that symmetry in their distortion, so to speak, which is less the characteristic of British than of Continental grotesques of the period, though all four were different from each other. A beholder was convinced that nothing on earth could be more hideous than those he saw on the south side – until he went round to the north. Of the two on this latter face, only that at the north-eastern corner concerns the story. It was too human to be called like a dragon, too impish to be like a man, too animal to be like a fiend, and not enough like a bird to be called a griffin. This horrible stone entity was fashioned as if covered with a wrinkled hide, it had short, erect ears, eyes starting from their sockets, and its fingers and hands were seizing the corners of its mouth, which they thus seemed to pull open to give freer passage to the water it vomited. The lower row of teeth was quite washed away, though the upper still remained. Here and thus, jutting a couple of feet from the wall against which its feet rested as a support, the creature had for four hundred years laughed at the surrounding landscape voicelessly in dry weather, and, in wet, with a gurgling and snorting sound.

Troy slept on in the porch, and the rain increased outside. Presently from the mouth of the gargoyle a small stream began to trickle through the seventy feet of aerial space between its head and the ground, which the water-drops smote like duckshot in their accelerated velocity. The stream thickened in substance, and increased in power, – gradually spouting further and yet further from the side of the tower. When the rain fell in a steady and ceaseless torrent, the stream dashed downward in volumes.

We follow its curve to the ground at this point of time. The base of the liquid parabola has come forward from the wall, has advanced over the plinth mouldings, over a heap of stones, over the marble border, into the midst of Fanny Robin's grave.

The force of the stream had until very lately been received upon some loose stones spread thereabout, which had acted as a shield to the soil under the onset. These during the summer had been cleared from the ground, and there was now nothing to resist the downfall but the bare earth. For several years the stream had not spouted so far from the tower as it was doing on this night, and such a contingency had been overlooked. Sometimes this obscure corner received no inhabitant for the space of two or three years, and then it was usually but a pauper, a poacher, or other sinner of undignified sins.

The persistent torrent from the gargoyle's jaws directed all its vengeance into the grave. The rich tawny mould was stirred into motion, and boiled like chocolate. The water accumulated and washed deeper down, and the roar of the pool thus formed spread into the night as the head and chief among other noises of the kind formed by the deluging rain. The flowers so carefully planted by Fanny's repentant lover began to move and turn in their bed. The heartsease turned slowly upside down, and became a mere mat of mud. Soon the snowdrop and other bulbs danced in the boiling mass like ingredients in a cauldron. Roots of the tufted species were loosened, rose to the surface, and floated off.

Troy did not awake from his comfortless sleep till it was broad day. Not having been in bed for two nights his shoulders felt stiff, his feet tender, and his head heavy. He remembered his position, arose, shivered, took the spade, and again went out.

The rain had quite ceased, and the sun was shining through the green, brown, and yellow leaves, now sparkling and varnished by the rain drops to the brightness of similar effects in the landscapes of Ruysdael and Hobbema, and full of all those infinite beauties that arise from the union of water and colour with high lights. The air was rendered so transparent by the heavy fall of rain that the autumn hues of the middle distance were as rich as those near at hand, and the distant fields intercepted by the angle of the tower appeared in the same plane as the tower itself.

He entered the gravel path which would take him behind the tower. The path, instead of being stony, as it had been the night before, was browned over with a thin coating of mud. At one place in the path he saw a tuft of stringy roots washed white and clean as a bundle of tendons. He picked it up – surely it could not be one of the primroses he had planted? He saw a bulb, another, and another as he advanced. Beyond doubt they were the crocuses. With a face of perplexed dismay Troy turned the corner and then beheld the wreck the stream had made.

The pool upon the grave had soaked away into the ground, and in its place was a hollow. The disturbed earth was washed over the grass and pathway in the guise of the brown mud he had already seen, and it spotted the marble tombstone with the same hues. Nearly all the flowers were washed clean out of the ground, and they lay, roots upwards, on the spots whither they had been floated by the stream.

Troy's brow became heavily contracted. He set his teeth closely, and his compressed lips moved as those of one in great pain. This trifling accident, by a strange confluence of emotions in him, was felt as the sharpest sting of all. Troy's face was very expressive, and any observer who had seen him now would hardly have believed him to be a man who had laughed, and sung, and poured love-trifles into a woman's ear. To curse his miserable lot was at first his impulse, but even that lowest stage of rebellion needed an activity whose absence was necessarily antecedent to the existence of the sort of misery he now endured. The sight, coming as it did, superimposed upon the other dark scenery of the previous days, formed a sort of climax to the whole panorama; and it was more than he could endure. Sanguine by nature, Troy had a power of eluding grief by simply adjourning it. He could put off the consideration of any particular spectre till the matter had become old and softened by time. The planting of flowers on Fanny's grave had been perhaps but a species of elusion of the primary grief, and now it was as if his intention had been known and circumvented.

Far from the Madding Crowd
Thomas Hardy (1840–1928)

Requiescat

Tread lightly, she is near
  Under the snow,
Speak gently, she can hear
  The daisies grow.

All her bright golden hair
  Tarnished with rust,
She that was young and fair
  Fallen to dust.

Lily-like, white as snow,
  She hardly knew
She was a woman, so
  Sweetly she grew.

Coffin board, heavy stone,
  Lie on her breast,
I vex my heart alone,
  She is at rest.

Peace, peace, she cannot hear
  Lyre or sonnet,
All my life's buried here,
  Heap earth upon it.

Oscar Wilde (1854–1900)

Remembrance

Cold in the earth – and the deep snow piled above thee,
Far, far removed, cold in the dreary grave!
Have I forgot, my only Love, to love thee,
Severed at last by Time's all-severing wave?

Now, when alone, do my thoughts no longer hover
Over the mountains, on that northern shore,
Resting their wings where heath and fern-leaves cover
Thy noble heart for ever, ever more?

Cold in the earth – and fifteen wild Decembers,
From those brown hills, have melted into spring:
Faithful, indeed, is the spirit that remembers
After such years of change and suffering!

Sweet Love of youth, forgive, if I forget thee,
While the world's tide is bearing me along;
Other desires and other hopes beset me,
Hopes which obscure, but cannot do thee wrong!

No later light has lightened up my heaven,
No second morn has ever shone for me;
All my life's bliss from thy dear life was given,
All my life's bliss is in the grave with thee.

But, when the days of golden dreams had perished,
And even Despair was powerless to destroy;
Then did I learn how existence could be cherished,
Strengthened, and fed without the aid of joy.

Then did I check the tears of useless passion –
Weaned my young soul from yearning after thine;
Sternly denied its burning wish to hasten
Down to that tomb already more than mine.

And, even yet, I dare not let it languish,
Dare not indulge in memory's rapturous pain;
Once drinking deep of that divinest anguish,
How could I seek the empty world again?

Emily Brontë (1818–48)

Rest

O Earth, lie heavily upon her eyes;
   Seal her sweet eyes weary of watching, Earth;
   Lie close around her; leave no room for mirth
With its harsh laughter, nor for sound of sighs.
She hath no questions, she hath no replies,
   Hushed in and curtained with a blessèd dearth
   Of all that irked her from the hour of birth;
With stillness that is almost Paradise.
Darkness more clear than noon-day holdeth her,
   Silence more musical than any song;
Even her very heart has ceased to stir:
Until the morning of Eternity
Her rest shall not begin nor end, but be;
   And when she wakes she will not think it long.

Christina Rossetti (1830–94)

On My First Son

Farewell, thou child of my right hand, and joy;
   My sin was too much hope of thee, loved boy.
Seven years thou wert lent to me, and I thee pay,
   Exacted by thy fate, on the just day.
Oh, could I lose all father now! For why
   Will man lament the state he should envy?
To have so soon 'scaped world's and flesh's rage,
   And if no other misery, yet age?
Rest in soft peace, and, asked, say here doth lie
   Ben Jonson his best piece of poetry;
For whose sake, henceforth, all his vows be such,
   As what he loves may never like too much.

Ben Jonson (*c.* 1572–1637)

The Widow at the Grave

She was looking at a humble stone which told of a young man who had died at twenty-three years old, fifty-five years ago, when she heard a faltering step approaching, and looking round saw a feeble woman bent with the weight of years, who tottered to the foot of that same grave and asked her to read the writing on the stone. The old woman thanked her when she had done, saying that she had had the words by heart for many a long, long year, but could not see them now.

'Were you his mother?' said the child.

'I was his wife, my dear.'

She was the wife of a young man of three-and-twenty! Ah, true! It was fifty-five years ago.

'You wonder to hear me say that,' remarked the old woman, shaking her head. 'You're not the first. Older folk than you have wondered at the same thing before now. Yes, I was his wife. Death doesn't change us more than life, my dear.'

'Do you come here often?' asked the child.

'I sit here very often in the summer time,' she answered; 'I used to come here once to cry and mourn, but that was a weary while ago, bless God!'

'I pluck the daisies as they grow, and take them home,' said the old woman after a short silence. 'I like no flowers so well as these, and haven't for five-and-fifty years. It's a long time, and I'm getting very old!'

Then growing garrulous upon a theme which was new to one listener though it were but a child, she told her how she had wept and moaned and prayed to die herself, when this happened; and how when she first came to that place, a young creature strong in love and grief, she had hoped that her heart was breaking as it seemed to be. But that time passed by, and although she continued to be sad when she came there, still she could bear to come, and so went on until it was pain no longer, but a solemn pleasure, and a duty she had learned to like. And now that five-and-fifty years were gone, she spoke of the dead man as if he had been her son or grandson, with a kind of pity for his youth, growing out of her own old age, and an exalting of his strength and manly beauty as compared with her own weakness and decay; and yet she spoke about him as her husband too, and thinking of herself in connection with him, as she used to be and not as she was now, talked of their meeting in another world, as if he were dead but yesterday, and she, separated from her former self, were thinking of the happiness of that comely girl who seemed to have died with him.

The Old Curiosity Shop
Charles Dickens (1812–70)

Parted

Farewell to one now silenced quite,
Sent out of hearing, out of sight, –
   My friend of friends, whom I shall miss.
   He is not banished, though, for this, –
Nor he, nor sadness, nor delight.

Though I shall talk with him no more,
A low voice sounds upon the shore.
   He must not watch my resting place
   But who shall drive a mournful face
From the sad winds about my door?

I shall not hear his voice complain
But who shall stop the patient rain?
   His tears must not disturb my heart,
   But who shall change the years, and part
The world from any thought of pain?

Although my life is left so dim,
The morning crowns the mountain rim;
   Joy is not gone from summer skies,
   Nor innocence from children's eyes,
And all these things are part of him.

He is not banished, for the showers
Yet wake this green warm earth of ours.
   How can the summer but be sweet?
   I shall not have him at my feet,
And yet my feet are on the flowers.

Alice Meynell (1847–1922)

O Captain! My Captain!

O Captain! my Captain! our fearful trip is done,
The ship has weathered every rack, the prize we sought is won,
The port is near, the bells I hear, the people all exulting,
While follow eyes the steady keel, the vessel grim and daring;
   But O heart! heart! heart!
      O the bleeding drops of red,
         Where on the deck my Captain lies,
         Fallen cold and dead.

O Captain! my Captain! rise up and hear the bells;
Rise up – for you the flag is flung – for you the bugle trills,
For you bouquets and ribboned wreaths – for you the shores
  a-crowding,
For you they call, the swaying mass, their eager faces turning;
   Here Captain! dear father!
      This arm beneath your head!
         It is some dream that on the deck,
         You've fallen cold and dead.

My Captain does not answer, his lips are pale and still,
My father does not feel my arm, he has no pulse nor will,
The ship is anchored safe and sound, its voyage closed and
done,
From fearful trip the victor ship comes in with object won:
   Exult O shores, and ring O bells!
      But I with mournful tread,
         Walk the deck my Captain lies,
         Fallen cold and dead.

Walt Whitman (1819–92)

Mater Dolorosa

I'd a dream tonight
  As I fell asleep,
O! the touching sight
  Makes me still to weep:
Of my little lad,
  Gone to leave me sad,
Ay, the child I had,
  But was not to keep.

As in heaven high,
  I my child did seek,
There in train came by
  Children fair and meek,
Each in lily white,
With a lamp alight;
Each was clear to sight,
  But they did not speak.

Then, a little sad,
  Came my child in turn,
But the lamp he had,
  O it did not burn!
He, to clear my doubt,
Said, half turned about,
'Your tears put it out;
  Mother, never mourn.'

William Barnes (1801–86)

Beeny Cliff

O the opal and the sapphire of that wandering western sea,
And the woman riding high above with bright hair flapping free –
The woman whom I loved so, and who loyally loved me.

The pale mews plained below us, and the waves seemed far away
In a nether sky, engrossed in saying their ceaseless babbling say,
As we laughed light-heartedly aloft on that clear-sunned March day.

A little cloud then cloaked us, and there flew an irised rain,
And the Atlantic dyed its levels with a dull misfeatured stain,
And then the sun burst out again, and purples prinked the main.

– Still in all its chasmal beauty bulks old Beeny to the sky,
And shall she and I not go there once again now March is nigh,
And the sweet things said in that March say anew there by and by?

What if still in chasmal beauty looms that wild weird western shore,
The woman now is – elsewhere – whom the ambling pony bore,
And nor knows nor cares for Beeny, and will laugh there never more.

Thomas Hardy (1840–1928)

In Memoriam VII

Dark house, by which once more I stand
   Here in the long unlovely street,
   Doors, where my heart was used to beat
So quickly, waiting for a hand,

A hand that can be clasped no more –
   Behold me, for I cannot sleep,
   And like a guilty thing I creep
At earliest morning to the door.

He is not here; but far away
   The noise of life begins again
   And ghastly through the drizzling rain
On the bald street breaks the blank day.

           Alfred, Lord Tennyson (1809–92)

In the Garden at Swainston

Nightingales warbled without,
    Within was weeping for thee:
Shadows of three dead men
    Walked in the walks with me:
Shadows of three dead men, and thou wast one of the three.

Nightingales sang in the woods:
    The Master was far away:
Nightingales warbled and sang
    Of a passion that lasts but a day;
Still in the house in his coffin the Prince of courtesy lay.

Two dead men have I known
    In courtesy like to thee:
Two dead men have I loved
    With a love that ever will be:
Three dead men have I loved, and thou art last of the three.

Alfred, Lord Tennyson (1809–92)

An Epitaph

O mortal folk, you may behold and see
How I lie here, sometime a mighty knight;
The end of joy and all prosperity
Is death at last, thorough his course and might:
After the day there cometh the dark night,
    For though the day be never so long,
    At last the bells ringeth to evensong.

Stephen Hawes (*c.*1475–1511)

An Epitaph

Upon a Young Married Couple Dead and Buried Together

To these, whom Death again did wed,
This grave's their second marriage bed;
For though the hand of Fate could force
'Twixt soul and body a divorce,
It could not sunder man and wife,
Because they both lived but one life.
Peace, good Reader, do not weep.
Peace, the lovers are asleep.
They, sweet turtles, folded lie
In the last knot Love could tie.
And though they lie as they were dead,
Their pillow stone, their sheets of lead,
(Pillow hard, and sheets not warm)
Love made the bed; they'll take no harm.
Let them sleep: let them sleep on,
Till the stormy night be gone,
Till the eternal morrow dawn;
Then the curtains will be drawn
And they wake into a light,
Whose day shall never die in night.

Richard Crashaw (*c.* 1612–49)

On a Favourite Cat, Drowned in a Tub of Gold Fishes

'Twas on a lofty vase's side,
Where China's gayest art had dyed
   The azure flowers that blow;
Demurest of the tabby kind,
The pensive Selima reclined,
   Gazed on the lake below.

Her conscious tail her joy declared;
The fair round face, the snowy beard,
   The velvet of her paws,
Her coat, that with the tortoise vies,
Her ears of jet, and emerald eyes,
   She saw; and purred applause.

Still had she gazed; but 'midst the tide
Two angel forms were seen to glide,
   The Genii of the stream:
Their scaly armour's Tyrian hue
Through richest purple to the view
   Betrayed a golden gleam.

The hapless Nymph with wonder saw:
A whisker first and then a claw,
   With many an ardent wish,
She stretched in vain to reach the prize.
What female heart can gold despise?
   What Cat's averse to fish?

Presumptuous Maid! with looks intent

Again she stretched, again she bent,
  Nor knew the gulf between.
(Malignant Fate sat by, and smiled.)
The slippery verge her feet beguiled,
  She tumbled headlong in.

Eight times emerging from the flood
She mewed to every watery god,
  Some speedy aid to send.
No Dolphin came, no Nereid stirred:
Nor cruel *Tom*, nor *Susan* heard.
  A Favourite has no friend!

From hence, ye Beauties undeceived,
Know, one false step is never retrieved,
  And be with caution bold.
Not all that tempts your wandering eyes
And heedless hearts, is lawful prize;
  Nor all that glisters, gold.

Thomas Gray (1716–71)

Death

It is not death, that sometime in a sigh
    This eloquent breath shall take its speechless flight;
That sometime these bright stars, that now reply
    In sunlight to the sun, shall set in night;
    That this warm conscious flesh shall perish quite,
And all life's ruddy springs forget to flow;
    That thoughts shall cease, and the immortal sprite
Be lapped in alien clay and laid below;
It is not death to know this – but to know
    That pious thoughts, which visit at new graves
In tender pilgrimage, will cease to go
    So duly and so oft – and when grass waves
Over the passed-away, there may be then
No resurrection in the minds of men.

                            Thomas Hood (1799–1845)

Funerals and
Death-Days

Ophelia's Death

There is a willow grows aslant a brook,
That shows his hoar leaves in the glassy stream;
There with fantastic garlands did she make,
Of crowflowers, nettles, daisies, and long purples,
That liberal shepherds give a grosser name,
But our cold maids do dead men's fingers call them.
There, on the pendent boughs her coronet weeds
Clambering to hang, an envious sliver broke;
When down her weedy trophies and herself
Fell in the weeping brook. Her clothes spread wide,
And, mermaid-like, awhile they bore her up;
Which time she chanted snatches of old tunes,
As one incapable of her own distress,
Or like a creature native and indued
Unto that element; but long it could not be
Till that her garments, heavy with their drink,
Pulled the poor wretch from her melodious lay,
To muddy death.

Hamlet, Act 4 Scene 7
William Shakespeare (1564–1616)

The Death of Little Nell

By little and little, the old man had drawn back towards the inner chamber, while these words were spoken. He pointed there, as he replied, with trembling lips.

'You plot among you to wean my heart from her. You never will do that –never while I have life. I have no relative or friend but her – I never had – I never will have. She is all in all to me. It is too late to part us now.'

Waving them off with his hand, and calling softly to her as he went, he stole into the room. They who were left behind, drew close together, and after a few whispered words – not unbroken by emotion, or easily uttered – followed him. They moved so gently, that their footsteps made no noise; but there were sobs from among the group, and sounds of grief and mourning.

For she was dead. There, upon her little bed, she lay at rest. The solemn stillness was no marvel now.

She was dead. No sleep so beautiful and calm, so free from trace of pain, so fair to look upon. She seemed a creature fresh from the hand of God, and waiting for the breath of life; not one who had lived and suffered death.

Her couch was dressed with here and there some winter berries and green leaves, gathered in a spot she had been used to favour.

'When I die, put near me something that has loved the light, and had the sky above it always.' Those were her words.

She was dead. Dear, gentle, patient, noble Nell, was dead. Her little bird – a poor slight thing the pressure of a finger would have crushed – was stirring nimbly in its cage;

and the strong heart of its child-mistress was mute and motionless for ever.

Where were the traces of her early cares, her sufferings, and fatigues? All gone. Sorrow was dead indeed in her, but peace and perfect happiness were born; imaged in her tranquil beauty and profound repose.

And still her former self lay there, unaltered in this change. Yes. The old fireside had smiled upon that same sweet face; it had passed, like a dream, through haunts of misery and care; at the door of the poor schoolmaster on the summer evening, before the furnace fire upon the cold wet night, at the still bedside of the dying boy, there had been the same mild lovely look. So shall we know the angels in their majesty, after death.

The old man held one languid arm in his, and had the small hand tight folded to his breast, for warmth. It was the hand she had stretched out to him with her last smile – the hand that had led him on through all their wanderings. Ever and anon he pressed it to his lips; then hugged it to his breast again, murmuring that it was warmer now; and as he said it he looked, in agony, to those who stood around, as if imploring them to help her.

She was dead, and past all help, or need of it. The ancient rooms she had seemed to fill with life, even while her own was waning fast – the garden she had tended – the eyes she had gladdened – the noiseless haunts of many a thoughtful hour – the paths she had trodden as it were but yesterday – could know her no more.

'It is not,' said the schoolmaster, as he bent down to kiss her on the cheek, and gave his tears free vent, 'it is not on earth that Heaven's justice ends. Think what it is, compared with the World to which her young spirit has winged its early flight, and say, if one deliberate wish expressed in solemn terms above this bed could call her back to life, which of us would utter it!'

The Old Curiosity Shop
Charles Dickens (1812–70)

The Death-Bed

We watched her breathing through the night,
    Her breathing soft and low,
As in her breast the wave of life
    Kept heaving to and fro.

So silently we seemed to speak,
    So slowly moved about,
As we had lent her half our powers
    To eke her living out.

Our very hopes belied our fears,
    Our fears our hopes belied –
We thought her dying when she slept,
    And sleeping when she died.

For when the morn came dim and sad,
    And chill with early showers,
Her quiet eyelids closed – she had
    Another morn than ours.

Thomas Hood (1799–1845)

The Death of Socrates

Now the hour of sunset was near, for a good deal of time had passed while he was within. When he came out, he sat down with us again after his bath, but not much was said. Soon the jailer, who was the servant of the Eleven, entered and stood by him, saying, 'To you, Socrates, whom I know to be the noblest and gentlest and best of all who ever came to this place, I will not impute the angry feelings of other men, who rage and swear at me, when, in obedience to the authorities, I bid them drink the poison – indeed, I am sure that you will not be angry with me; for others, as you are aware, and not I, are to blame. And so fare you well, and try to bear lightly what must needs be – you know my errand.' Then bursting into tears he turned away and went out.

Socrates looked at him and said, 'I return your good wishes, and will do as you bid.' Then turning to us, he said, 'How charming the man is: since I have been in prison he has always been coming to see me, and at times he would talk to me, and was as good to me as could be, and now see how generously he sorrows on my account. We must do as he says, Crito; and therefore let the cup be brought, if the poison is prepared: if not, let the attendant prepare some.'

'Yet,' said Crito, 'the sun is still upon the hill tops, and I know that many a one has taken the draught late, and after the announcement has been made to him, he has eaten and drunk, and enjoyed the society of his beloved; do not hurry – there is time enough.'

Socrates said, 'Yes, Crito, and they of whom you speak are right in so acting, for they think that they will be gainers by the delay; but I am right in not following their example, for I do not think that I should gain anything by drinking the poison a little later; I should only be ridiculous in my own eyes for sparing and saving a life which is already forfeit. Please then to do as I say, and not to refuse me.'

Crito made a sign to the servant, who was standing by; and he went out, and having been absent for some time, returned with the jailer carrying the cup of poison. Socrates said, 'You, my good friend, who are experienced in these matters, shall give me directions how I am to proceed.' The man answered, 'You have only to walk about until your legs are heavy, and then to lie down, and the poison will act.' At the same time he handed the cup to Socrates, who in the easiest and gentlest manner, without the least fear or change of colour or feature, looking at the man with all his eyes, as his manner was, took the cup and said, 'What do you say about making a libation out of this cup to any god? May I, or not?' The man answered, 'We only prepare, Socrates, just so much as we deem enough.'

'I understand,' he said, 'but I may and must ask the gods to prosper my journey from this to the other world – even so – and so be it according to my prayer.' Then raising the cup to his lips, quite readily and cheerfully he drank off the poison. And hitherto most of us had been able to control our sorrow; but now when we saw him drinking, and saw too that he had finished the draught, we could not longer forbear, and in spite of myself my own tears were flowing fast; so that I covered my face and wept, not for him, but at the thought of my own calamity in having to part from such a friend. Nor was I the first; for Crito, when he found himself unable to restrain his tears, had got up, and I followed; and at that moment, Apollodorus, who had been weeping all the time, broke out in a loud and passionate cry which made cowards of us all. Socrates alone retained his calmness. 'What is this strange outcry?' he said. 'I sent away the women mainly in order that they might not misbehave in this way, for I have been told that a man should die in peace. Be quiet then, and have patience.' When we heard his words we were ashamed, and refrained our tears; and he walked about until, as he said, his legs began to fail, and then he lay on his back, according to the directions, and the man who gave him the poison now and then looked at his feet and legs; and after a while he pressed his foot hard, and asked him if he could feel; and he said, 'No'; and then his leg, and so upwards and upwards, and showed us that he was cold and stiff. And he felt them himself, and said, 'When the poison reaches the heart, that will be the end.' He was beginning to grow cold about the groin, when he uncovered his face, for he had covered himself up, and said – they were his last words – he said, 'Crito, I owe a cock to Asclepius; will you remember to pay the debt?'

'The debt shall be paid,' said Crito; 'Is there anything else?' There was no answer to this question; but in a minute or two a movement was heard, and the attendants uncovered him; his eyes were set, and Crito closed his eyes and mouth.

Such was the end of our friend; concerning whom I may truly say, that of all the men of his time whom I have known, he was the wisest and justest and best.

Plato (*c.* 428–348 BC)
Translated by Benjamin Jowett (1817–93)

The Flood

For the first time Maggie's heart began to beat in an agony of dread. She sat helpless – dimly conscious that she was being floated along – more intensely conscious of the anticipated clash. But the horror was transient: it passed away before the oncoming warehouses of St. Ogg's: she had passed the mouth of the Ripple, then: *now*, she must use all her skill and power to manage the boat and get it if possible out of the current. She could see now that the bridge was broken down; she could see the masts of a stranded vessel far out over the watery field. But no boats were to be seen moving on the river – such as had been laid hands on were employed in the flooded streets.

With new resolution, Maggie seized her oar, and stood up again to paddle; but the now ebbing tide added to the swiftness of the river, and she was carried along beyond the bridge. She could hear shouts from the windows overlooking the river, as if the people there were calling to her. It was not till she had passed on nearly to Tofton that she could get the boat clear of the current. Then with one yearning look towards her uncle Deane's house that lay farther down the river she took to both her oars and rowed with all her might across the watery fields, back toward the Mill. Colour was beginning to awake now, and as she approached the Dorlcote fields, she could discern the tints of the trees – could see the old Scotch firs far to the right, and the home chestnuts – Oh! how deep they lay in the water: deeper than the trees on this side the hill. And the roof of the Mill – where was it? Those heavy fragments hurrying down the Ripple – what had they meant? But it was not the house – the house stood firm: drowned up to the first story, but still firm – or was it broken in at the end towards the Mill?

With panting joy that she was there at last – joy that overcame all distress, Maggie neared the front of the house. At first she heard no sound; she saw no object moving. Her boat was on a level with the upstairs windows. She called out in a loud, piercing voice, 'Tom, where are you? Mother, where are you? Here is Maggie!'

Soon, from the window of the attic in the central gable, she heard Tom's voice: 'Who is it? Have you brought a boat?'

'It is I, Tom – Maggie. Where is Mother?'

'She is not here: she went to Garum, the day before yesterday. I'll come down to the lower window.'

'Alone, Maggie?' said Tom, in a voice of deep astonishment, as he opened the middle window on a level with the boat.

'Yes, Tom: God has taken care of me, to bring me to you. Get in quickly. Is there no one else?'

'No,' said Tom, stepping into the boat. 'I fear the man is drowned: he was carried down the Ripple, I think, when part of the mill fell with the crash of trees and stones against it: I've shouted again and again, and there has been no answer. Give me the oars, Maggie.'

It was not till Tom had pushed off and they were on the wide water – he face to face with Maggie – that the full meaning of what had happened rushed upon his mind. It came with so overpowering a force – it was such a new revelation to his spirit, of the depths in life, that had lain beyond his vision, which he had fancied so keen and clear –

that he was unable to ask a question. They sat mutely gazing at each other: Maggie with eyes of intense life looking out from a weary, beaten face – Tom pale, with a certain awe and humiliation. Thought was busy though the lips were silent: and though he could ask no question, he guessed a story of almost miraculous, divinely-protected effort. But at last a mist gathered over the blue-grey eyes, and the lips found a word they could utter: the old childish – 'Magsie!'

Maggie could make no answer but a long deep sob of that mysterious, wondrous happiness that is one with pain.

As soon as she could speak, she said, 'We will go to Lucy, Tom: we'll go and see if she is safe, and then we can help the rest.'

Tom rowed with untired vigour, and with a different speed from poor Maggie's. The boat was soon in the current of the river again, and soon they would be at Tofton.

'Park House stands high up out of the flood,' said Maggie. 'Perhaps they have got Lucy there.'

Nothing else was said; a new danger was being carried towards them by the river. Some wooden machinery had just given way on one of the wharves, and huge fragments were being floated along. The sun was rising now, and the wide area of watery desolation was spread out in dreadful clearness around them – in dreadful clearness floated onwards the hurrying, threatening masses. A large company in a boat that was working its way along under the Tofton houses, observed their danger, and shouted, 'Get out of the current!'

But that could not be done at once; and Tom, looking before him, saw death rushing on them. Huge fragments, clinging together in fatal fellowship, made one wide mass across the stream.

'It is coming, Maggie!' Tom said, in a deep hoarse voice, loosing the oars, and clasping her.

The next instant the boat was no longer seen upon the water – and the huge mass was hurrying on in hideous triumph.

But soon the keel of the boat reappeared, a black speck on the golden water.

The boat reappeared – but brother and sister had gone down in an embrace never to be parted: living through again in one supreme moment the days when they had clasped their little hands in love, and roamed the daisied fields together.

The Mill on the Floss
George Eliot (1819–80)

Shameful Death

There were four of us about that bed;
　The mass-priest knelt at the side,
I and his mother stood at the head,
　Over his feet lay the bride;
We were quite sure that he was dead,
　Though his eyes were open wide.

He did not die in the night,
　He did not die in the day,
But in the morning twilight
　His spirit passed away,
When neither sun nor moon was bright,
　And the trees were merely grey.

He was not slain with the sword,
　Knight's axe, or the knightly spear,
Yet spoke he never a word
　After he came in here;
I cut away the cord
　From the neck of my brother dear.

He did not strike one blow,
　For the recreants came behind,
In the place where the hornbeams grow,
　A path right hard to find,
For the hornbeam boughs swing so,
　That the twilight makes it blind.

They lighted a great torch then,
　　When his arms were pinioned fast,
Sir John the night of the Fen,
　　Sir Guy of the Dolorous Blast,
With knights threescore and ten,
　　Hung brave Lord Hugh at last.

I am threescore and ten,
　　And my hair is all turned grey,
But I met Sir John of the Fen,
　　Long ago on a summer day,
And am glad to think of the moment when
　　I took his life away.

I am threescore and ten,
　　And my strength is mostly passed,
But long ago I and my men,
　　When the sky was overcast,
And the smoke rolled over the reeds of the fen,
　　Slew Guy of the Dolorous Blast.

And now, knights all of you,
　　I pray you pray for Sir Hugh,
A good knight and a true,
　　And for Alice, his wife, pray too.

William Morris (1834–96)

A Death-Day Recalled

Beeny did not quiver,
　　Juliot grew not gray,
Thin Vallency's river
　　Held its wonted way.
Bos seemed not to utter
　　Dimmest note of dirge,
Targan mouth a mutter
　　To its creamy surge.

Yet though these, unheeding,
　　Listless, passed the hour
Of her spirit's speeding,
　　She had, in her flower,
Sought and loved the places –
　　Much and often pined
For their lonely faces
　　When in towns confined.

Why did not Vallency
　　In his purl deplore
One whose haunts were whence he
　　Drew his limpid store?
Why did Bos not thunder
　　Targan apprehend
Body and Breath were sunder
　　Of their former friend?

Thomas Hardy (1840–1928)

Proserpine and Dis

Near Enna walls there stands a lake: Pergusa is the name.
Cayster heareth not more songs of swans than doth the same.
A word environs every side the water round about,
And with his leaves as with a veil doth keep the sun's heat out.
The boughs do yield a cool fresh air: the moistness of the ground
Yields sundry flowers: continual spring is all the year there found.
While in this garden Proserpine was taking her pastime,
In gathering either violets blue, or lilies white as lime,
And while of maidenly desire she filled her mind and lap,
Endeavouring to outgather her companions there. By hap
Dis spied her, loved her, caught her up, and all at once well near,
So hasty, hot and swift a thing is love, as may appear
The lady with a wailing voice afright did often call
Her mother and her waiting maids, but mother most of all.
And as she from the upper part of her garment would have rent,
By chance she let her lap slip down, and out the flowers went.
And such a silly simpleness her childish age yet bears,
That even the very loss of them did move her more to tears.

Metamorphosis V
Ovid (43 BC–AD 18)
Translated by Arthur Golding (*c.* 1536–1605)

Mourning Sir Lancelot

And so the bishop and they all together went with the body of Sir Lancelot daily till they came to Joyous Garde, and ever they had a hundred torches burning above him.

And so, within 15 days they came to Joyous Garde. And there they laid his corpse in the body of the choir, and sang and read many psalms and prayers over him and about him, and ever his visage was laid open and naked that all folks might behold him. For such was the custom in those days that all men of worship should so lie with open visage till they were buried. And right thus as they were at their service there came Sir Hector de Maris, that had seven years sought all England, Scotland and Wales seeking his brother Sir Lancelot.

And when Sir Hector heard such noise and light in the choir of Joyous Garde he alight and put his horse from him and came in to the choir. And there he saw men sing and weep, and all they knew Sir Hector but he knew not them.

Then went Sir Bors unto Sir Hector and told him how there lay his brother, Sir Lancelot, dead. And then Sir Hector threw his shield, sword and helmet from him and when he beheld Sir Lancelot's visage he fell down in a swoon. And when he waked it hard any tongue to tell the doleful complaints he made for his brother.

'Ah Lancelot,' he said, 'thou were head of all Christian knights!

'And now I dare say,' said Sir Hector, 'thou Sir Lancelot, there thou lyest, that thou were never matched of earthly knight's hand. And thou were the most courteous knight that ever bore shield. And thou were the truest friend to thy lover that ever bestrode horse, and thou were the truest lover, of a sinful man, that ever loved woman, and thou were the kindest man that ever struck with sword. And thou were the godliest person that ever came among preys of knights, and thou wert the meekest man and the gentlest that ever ate in halls among ladies, and thou wert the sternest knight to thy mortal foe that ever put spear in the rest.'

Then there was weeping and dolour out of measure.

Then they kept Sir Lancelot's corpse on-loft 15 days, and then they buried it with great devotion. And then at leisure they went all with the Bishop of Canterbury to his hermitage, and there they were together more than a month.

Le Morte D'Arthur
Book 21: The Death of Arthur
Sir Thomas Malory (d. 1471)

Casey Jones

Come all ye rounders, for I want you to hear
The story told of an engineer;
Casey Jones was the rounder's name,
With a heavy eight-wheeler of a mighty fame.

Caller called Jones about half past four,
He kissed his wife at the station door,
Climbed into the cab with the orders in his hand,
Says, 'This is my trip to the Holy land.'

Through South Memphis yards on the fly,
Heard the fireman say, 'You've got a white eye.'
All the switchmen knew by the engine moan
That the hogger at the throttle was Casey Jones.

The rain was coming down five or six weeks,
The railroad track was like the bed of a creek.
They rated him down to a thirty mile gait,
Threw the southbound mail about eight hours late.

Fireman says, 'Casey, you're running too fast,
You run that block board, the last station you passed.'
Jones says, 'Yes, I believe we'll make it, though,
For she steams a lot better than I ever know.'

Casey says, 'Fireman, don't you fret;
Keep knocking at the fire door, don't give up yet,
I'm going to run her till she leaves the rail,
Or make it on time with the Southern mail.'

Well, it was early in the morning when it looked like rain,
Around the bend came a passenger train.
Fireman hollered, 'Casey, it's just ahead,
We might jump and make it but we'll all be dead.'

Around the curve and down the dump,
Two locomotives were bound to bump.
Fireman jumped off, but Casey stayed on –
He's a good engineer, but he's dead and gone.

Well, poor Casey Jones, he was all right.
He stuck to his duty both day and night.
They loved to hear his whistle and his ring of Number 3,
As he came into Memphis on the old I.C.

Mrs. Casey Jones was sitting on the bed.
Telegram came that Casey is dead.
Says, 'Children, go to bed and hush your cryin',
You've got another papa on the 'Frisco line.'

Anon. (early 20th century)

Casabianca

The boy stood on the burning deck,
    Whence all but he had fled;
The flame that lit the battle's wreck
    Shone round him over the dead.

Yet beautiful and bright he stood,
    As born to rule the storm;
A creature of heroic blood,
    A proud though childlike form.

The flames rolled on – he would not go
    Without his father's word;
That father, faint in death below,
    His voice no longer heard.

He called aloud – 'Say, father, say
    If yet my task be done!'
He knew not that the chieftain lay
    Unconscious of his son.

'Speak, father!' once again he cried,
    'If I may yet be gone;'
And but the booming shots replied,
    And fast the flames rolled on.

Upon his brow he felt their breath,
    And in his waving hair,
And looked from that lone post of death
    In still yet brave despair.

And shouted but once more aloud,
  'My father, must I stay?'
While o'er him fast, through sail and shroud,
  The wreathing fires made way.

They wrapped the ship in splendour wild,
  They caught the flag on high,
And streamed above the gallant child,
  Like banners in the sky.

Then came a burst of thunder-sound –
  The boy! – oh, where was he?
Ask of the winds, that far around
  With fragments strewed the sea! –

With mast, and helm, and pennon fair,
  That well had borne their part;
But the noblest thing that perished there
  Was that young faithful heart.

Felicia Hemans (1793–1835)

Funeral of George II
Letter to George Montagu, 13 November 1760

Do you know, I had the curiosity to go to the burying t'other night; I had never seen a royal funeral; nay, I walked as a rag of quality, which I found would be, and so it was, the easiest way of seeing it. It is absolutely a noble sight. The Prince's chamber, hung with purple, and a quantity of silver lamps, the coffin under a canopy of purple velvet, and six vast chandeliers of silver on high stands, had a very good effect. The Ambassador from Tripoli and his son were carried to see that chamber. The procession through a line of foot-guards, every seventh man bearing a torch, the horse-guards lining the outside, their officers with drawn sabres and crape sashes on horseback, the drums muffled, the fifes, bells tolling, and minute guns, all this was very solemn. But the charm was the entrance of the Abbey, where we were received by the Dean and Chapter in rich robes, the choir and almsmen all bearing torches; the whole Abbey so illu-minated, that one saw it to greater advantage than by day; the tombs, long aisles, and fretted roof, all appearing dis-tinctly, and with the happiest chiaroscuro. There wanted nothing but incense, and little chapels here and there, with priests saying mass for the repose of the defunct – yet one could not complain of its not being Catholic enough. I had been in dread of being coupled with some boy of ten years old – but the heralds were not very accurate, and I walked with George Grenville, taller and older enough to keep me in countenance. When we came to the chapel of Henry the Seventh, all solemnity and decorum ceased – no order was observed, people sat or stood where they could or would, the yeomen of the guard were crying out for help, oppressed by the immense weight of the coffin, the Bishop read sadly, and blundered in the prayers, the fine chapter, *Man that is born of a woman*, was chanted, not read, and the anthem, besides being immeasurably tedious, would have served as well for a nuptial. The real serious part was the figure of the Duke of Cumberland, heightened by a thousand melancholy circumstances. He had a dark brown adonis, and a cloak of black cloth, with a train of five yards. Attending the funeral of a father, however little reason he had so to love him, could not be pleasant. His leg extremely bad, yet forced to stand upon it near two hours, his face bloated and distorted with his late paralytic stroke, which has affected, too, one of his eyes, and placed over the mouth of the vault, into which, in all probability, he must himself so soon descend – think how unpleasant a situation! He bore it all with a firm and unaffected countenance. This grave scene was fully contrasted by the burlesque Duke of Newcastle. He fell into a fit of crying the moment he came into the chapel, and flung himself back in a stall, the Archbishop hovering over him with a smelling-bottle – but in two minutes his curiosity got the better of his hypocrisy, and he ran about the chapel with his glass to spy who was or was not there, spying with one hand, and mopping his eyes with the t'other. Then returned the fear of catching cold, and the Duke of Cumberland, who was sinking with heat, felt himself weighed down, and turning round, found it was the Duke of Newcastle standing upon his train to avoid the chill of the marble. It was very theatric to look down into the vault, where the coffin lay, attended by mourners with lights. Clavering, the Groom of the Bedchamber, refused to sit up with the body, and was dismissed by the King's order.

Horace Walpole (1717–97)

London in Plague Time

The face of London was now indeed strangely altered, I mean the whole mass of buildings, city, liberties, suburbs, Westminster, Southwark, and altogether; for, as to the particular part called the city, or within the walls, that was not yet much infected; but in the whole, the face of things, I say, was much altered; sorrow and sadness sat upon every face, and though some parts were not yet overwhelmed, yet all looked deeply concerned; and as we saw it apparently coming on, so every one looked on himself, and his family, as in the utmost danger: were it possible to represent those times exactly, to those that did not see them, and give the reader due ideas of the horror that everywhere presented itself, it must make just impressions upon their minds, and fill them with surprise. London might well be said to be all in tears! The mourners did not go about the streets indeed, for nobody put on black, or made a formal dress of mourning for their nearest friends; but the voice of mourning was truly heard in the streets; the shrieks of women and children at the windows and doors of their houses, where their dearest relations were, perhaps dying, or just dead, were so frequent to be heard, as we passed the streets, that it was enough to pierce the stoutest heart in the world to hear them. Tears and lamentations were seen almost in every house, especially in the first part of the visitation; for towards the latter end, men's hearts were hardened, and death was so always before their eyes, that they did not so much concern themselves for the loss of their friends, expecting that themselves should be summoned the next hour.

A Journal of the Plague Year
Daniel Defoe (1660–1731)

Because I Could Not Stop for Death

Because I could not stop for Death –
He kindly stopped for me –
The Carriage held but just Ourselves –
And Immortality.

We slowly drove – He knew no haste
And I had put away
My labour and my leisure too,
For His Civility –

We passed the School, where Children strove
At Recess – in the Ring –
We passed the Fields of Gazing Grain –
We passed the Setting Sun –

Or rather – He passed Us –
The Dews drew quivering and chill –
For only Gossamer, my Gown –
My Tippet – only Tulle –

We paused before a House that seemed
A Swelling of the Ground –
The Roof was scarcely visible –
The Cornice – in the Ground –

Since then – 'tis Centuries – and yet
Feels shorter than the Day
I first surmised the Horses' Heads
Were toward Eternity –

Emily Dickinson (1830–86)

Sing No Sad Songs

Dirge

Come away, come away, death,
 And in sad cypress let me be laid.
Fly away, fly away, breath;
 I am slain by a fair cruel maid.
My shroud of white, stuck all with yew,
  Oh, prepare it!
My part of death, no one so true
  Did share it.

Not a flower, not a flower sweet,
 On my black coffin let there be strown;
Not a friend, not a friend greet
 My poor corpse, where my bones shall be thrown:
A thousand thousand sighs to save,
  Lay me, Oh, where
Sad true lover never find my grave,
  To weep there!

Twelfth Night, Act 2 Scene 4
William Shakespeare (1564–1616)

Song

When I am dead, my dearest,
Sing no sad songs for me;
Plant thou no roses at my head,
Nor shady cypress tree:
Be the green grass above me
With showers and dewdrops wet;
And if thou wilt, remember,
And if thou wilt, forget.

I shall not see the shadows,
I shall not feel the rain;
I shall not hear the nightingale
Sing on, as if in pain;
And dreaming through the twilight
That doth not rise nor set,
Haply I may remember,
And haply may forget.

Christina Rossetti (1830–94)

Come Not, When I Am Dead

Come not, when I am dead,
  To drop thy foolish tears upon my grave,
To trample round my fallen head,
  And vex the unhappy dust thou wouldst not save.
There let the wind sweep and the plover cry;
  But thou, go by.

Child, if it were thine error or thy crime
  I care no longer, being all unblest:
Wed whom thou wilt, but I am sick of Time,
  And I desire to rest.
Pass on, weak heart, and leave me where I lie:
  Go by, go by.

Alfred, Lord Tennyson (1809–92)

Requiem

Under the wide and starry sky,
Dig the grave and let me lie.
Glad did I live and gladly die,
   And I laid me down with a will.

This be the verse you grave for me:
Here he lies where he longed to be;
Home is the sailor, home from sea,
   And the hunter home from the hill.

Robert Louis Stevenson (1850–94)

Sonnet 71

No longer mourn for me when I am dead
Than you shall hear the surly sullen bell
Give warning to the world that I am fled
From this vile world, with vilest worms to dwell.
Nay, if you read this line, remember not
The hand that writ it, for I love you so,
That I in your sweet thoughts would be forgot
If thinking on me then should make you woe.
O, if, I say, you look upon this verse
When I perhaps compounded am with clay,
Do not so much as my poor name rehearse,
But let your love even with my life decay,
   Lest the wise world should look into your moan
   And mock you with me after I am gone.

William Shakespeare (1564–1616)

Crossing the Bar

Sunset and evening star,
   And one clear call for me!
And may there be no moaning of the bar,
   When I put out to sea,

But such a tide as moving seems asleep,
   Too full for sound and foam,
When that which drew from out the boundless deep
   Turns again home.

Twilight and evening bell,
   And after that the dark!
And may there be no sadness of farewell,
   When I embark;

For though from out our bourne of Time and Place
   The flood may bear me far,
I hope to see my Pilot face to face
   When I have crossed the bar.

Alfred, Lord Tennyson (1809–92)

When Death to Either Shall Come

When Death to either shall come, –
   I pray it be first to me, –
Be happy as ever at home,
   If so, as I wish, it be.

Possess thy heart, my own;
   And sing to the child on thy knee,
Or read to thyself alone
   The songs that I made for thee.

Robert Bridges (1844–1930)

The Funeral

Whoever comes to shroud me, do not harm
     Nor question much
That subtle wreath of hair about mine arm;
The mystery, the sign you must not touch,
     For 'tis my outward soul,
Viceroy to that which, unto heaven being gone,
     Will leave this to control
And keep these limbs, her provinces, from dissolution.

For if the sinewy thread my brain lets fall
     Through every part
Can tie those parts, and make me one of all,
Those hairs, which upward grew, and strength and art
     Have from a better brain,
Can better do't: except she meant that I
     By this should know my pain,
As prisoners then are manacled, when they're condemned
  to die.

Whate'er she meant by't, bury it with me,
     For since I am
Love's martyr, it might breed idolatry
If into other hands these relics came.
     As 'twas humility
T'afford to it all that a soul can do,
     So 'tis some bravery
That, since you would have none of me, I bury some of you.

                John Donne (1572–1631)

In After Days
Rondeau

In after days when grasses high
O'ertop the stone where I shall lie,
    Though ill or well the world adjust
    My slender claim to honoured dust,
I shall not question nor reply.

I shall not see the morning sky;
I shall not hear the night wind sigh;
    I shall be mute, as all men must
        In after days!

But yet, now living, fain would I
That someone then should testify,
    Saying – 'He held his pen in trust
    To Art, not serving shame or lust.'
Will none? – Then let my memory die
        In after days!

Henry Austin Dobson (1840–1921)

Afterwards

When the Present has latched its postern behind my tremulous stay,
    And the May month flaps its glad green leaves like wings,
Delicate-filmed as new-spun silk, will the neighbours say,
    'He was a man who used to notice such things'?

If it be in the dusk when, like an eyelid's soundless blink,
    The dewfall-hawk comes crossing the shades to alight
Upon the wind-warped upland thorn, a gazer may think,
    'To him this must have been a familiar sight.'

If I pass during some nocturnal blackness, mothy and warm,
    When the hedgehog travels furtively over the lawn,
One may say, 'He strove that such innocent creatures should
    come to no harm,
    But he could do little for them; and now he is gone.'

If, when hearing that I have been stilled at last, they stand at the
    door,
    Watching the full-starred heavens that winter sees,
Will this thought rise on those who will meet my face no more,
    'He was one who had an eye for such mysteries'?

And will any say when my bell of quittance is heard in the gloom,
    And a crossing breeze cuts a pause in its outrollings,
Till they rise again, as they were a new bell's boom,
    'He hears it not now, but used to notice such things'?

Thomas Hardy (1840–1928)

Death, Thou Shalt Die

Death, Be Not Proud

Death, be not proud, though some have called thee
Mighty and dreadful, for thou art not so:
For those whom thou think'st thou dost overthrow
Die not, poor Death; nor yet canst thou kill me.
From Rest and Sleep, which but thy pictures be,
Much pleasure, then from thee much more must flow;
And soonest our best men with thee do go –
Rest of their bones, and souls' delivery.
Thou'rt slave to fate, chance, kings, and desperate men,
And dost with poison, war, and sickness dwell;
And poppy or charms can make us sleep as well
And better than thy stroke. Why swell'st thou then?
One short sleep past, we wake eternally,
And Death shall be no more: Death, thou shalt die.

John Donne (1572–1631)

The Dying Christian to His Soul

Vital spark of heavenly flame,
Quit, oh quit this mortal frame:
Trembling, hoping, lingering, flying –
Oh the pain, the bliss of dying!
Cease, fond Nature, cease thy strife,
And let me languish into life!

Hark! they whisper; angels say,
Sister spirit, come away!
What is this absorbs me quite?
Steals my senses, shuts my sight,
Drowns my spirits, draws my breath?
Tell me, my soul, can this be death?

The world recedes; it disappears!
Heaven opens on my eyes! my ears
With sounds seraphic ring:
Lend, lend your wings: I mount! I fly!
O Grave! where is thy victory?
O Death! where is thy sting?

Alexander Pope (1688–1744)

No Worst, There Is None

No worst, there is none. Pitched past pitch of grief,
More pangs will, schooled at forepangs, wilder wring.
Comforter, where, where is your comforting?
Mary, mother of us, where is your relief?
My cries heave, herds-long; huddle in a main, a chief
Woe, world-sorrow; on an age-old anvil wince and sing –
Then lull, then leave off. Fury had shrieked 'No ling-
ering! Let me be fell: force I must be brief'.

  O the mind, mind has mountains; cliffs of fall
Frightful, sheer, no-man-fathomed. Hold them cheap
May who ne'er hung there. Nor does long our small
Durance deal with that steep or deep. Here! creep,
Wretch, under a comfort serves in a whirlwind: all
Life death does end and each day dies with sleep.

                Gerald Manley Hopkins (1844–89)

No Coward Soul Is Mine

No coward soul is mine
No trembler in the world's storm-troubled sphere:
I see Heaven's glories shine,
And Faith shines equal arming me from Fear.

O God within my breast,
Almighty ever-present Deity!
Life, that in me has rest,
As I Undying Life, have power in Thee!

Vain are the thousand creeds
That move men's hearts, unutterably vain,
Worthless as withered weeds,
Or idlest froth amid the boundless main,

To waken doubt in one
Holding so fast by thy infinity,
So surely anchored on
The steadfast rock of Immortality.

With wide-embracing love
Thy spirit animates eternal years,
Pervades and broods above,
Changes, sustains, dissolves, creates, and rears.

Though earth and moon were gone,
And suns and universes ceased to be,
And thou wert left alone,
Every existence would exist in thee.

There is not room for Death
Nor atom that his might could render void:
Since thou art Being and Breath,
And what thou art may never be destroyed.

Emily Brontë (1818–48)

Dirge for Fidele

Fear no more the heat o'the sun,
   Nor the furious winter's rages;
Thou thy worldly task hast done,
   Home art gone, and ta'en thy wages.
Golden lads and girls all must,
As chimney-sweepers, come to dust.

Fear no more the frown o'the great,
   Thou art past the tyrant's stroke;
Care no more to clothe and eat,
   To thee the reed is as the oak:
The sceptre, learning, physic, must
All follow this, and come to dust.

Fear no more the lightning flash,
   Nor the all-dreaded thunderstone;
Fear not slander, censure rash;
   Thou hast finished joy and moan.
All lovers young, all lovers must
Consign to thee, and come to dust.

No exorciser harm thee!
Nor no witchcraft charm thee!
Ghost unlaid forbear thee!
Nothing ill come near thee!
Quiet consummation have,
And renownèd be thy grave!

Cymbeline, Act 4 Scene 2
William Shakespeare (1564–1616)

Nothingness

After death nothing is, and nothing death;
The utmost limits of a gasp of breath.
Let the ambitious zealot lay aside
His hopes of Heaven (whose faith is but his pride);
Let slavish souls lay by their fear,
Nor be concerned which way, or where,
After this life they shall be hurled:
Dead, we become the lumber of the world,
And to that mass of matter shall be swept,
Where things destroyed with things unborn are kept;
Devouring Time swallows us whole,
Impartial Death confounds body and soul.
For Hell and the foul fiend that rules
    The everlasting fiery goals,
Devised by rogues, dreaded by fools,
With his grim, gisly dog that keeps the door,
    Are senseless stories, idle tales,
Dreams, whimsies, and no more.

Seneca (*c.* 4 BC–AD 65)
Translated by John Wilmot, Earl of Rochester (1647–80)

Sonnet 20

Poor soul, the centre of my sinful earth –
My sinful earth, these rebel powers array –
Why dost thou pine within and suffer dearth,
Painting thy outward walls so costly gay?
Why so large cost, having so short a lease,
Dost thou upon thy fading mansion spend?
Shall worms, inheritors of this excess,
Eat up thy charge? Is this thy body's end?
Then, soul, live thou upon thy servant's loss,
And let that pine to aggravate thy store;
Buy terms divine in selling hours of dross;
Within be fed, without be rich no more:
   So shalt thou feed on Death, that feeds on men;
   And Death once dead, there's no more dying then.

William Shakespeare (1564–1616)

Death

Death! that struck when I was most confiding
In my certain faith of joy to be –
Strike again, Time's withered branch dividing
From the fresh root of Eternity!

Leaves, upon Time's branch, were growing brightly,
Full of sap, and full of silver dew;
Birds beneath its shelter gathered nightly;
Daily round its flowers the wild bees flew.

Sorrow passed, and plucked the golden blossom;
Guilt stripped off the foliage in its pride;
But, within its parent's kindly bosom,
Flowed for ever Life's restoring tide.

Little mourned I for the parted gladness,
For the vacant nest and silent song –
Hope was there, and laughed me out of sadness;
Whispering, 'Winter will not linger long!'

And, behold! with tenfold increase blessing,
Spring adorned the beauty-burdened spray;
Wind and rain and fervent heat, caressing,
Lavished glory on that second May!

High it rose – no winged grief could sweep it;
Sin was scared to distance with its shine;
Love, and its own life, had power to keep it
From all wrong – from every blight but thine!

Cruel Death! The young leaves droop and languish;
Evening's gentle air may still restore –
No! the morning sunshine mocks my anguish –
Time, for me, must never blossom more!

Strike it down, that other boughs may flourish
Where that perished sapling used to be;
Thus, at least, its mouldering corpse will nourish
That from which it sprung – Eternity.

Emily Brontë (1818–48)

Endymion

A thing of beauty is a joy for ever:
Its loveliness increases; it will never
Pass into nothingness; but still will keep
A bower quiet for us, and a sleep
Full of sweet dreams, and health, and quiet breathing.
Therefore, on every morrow, are we wreathing
A flowery band to bind us to the earth,
Spite of despondence, of the inhuman dearth
Of noble natures, of the gloomy days,
Of all the unhealthy and o'er-darkened ways
Made for our searching: yes, in spite of all,
Some shape of beauty moves away the pall
From our dark spirits. Such the sun, the moon,
Trees old, and young, sprouting a shady boon
For simple sheep; and such are daffodils
With the green world they live in; and clear rills
That for themselves a cooling covert make
'Gainst the hot season; the mid forest brake,
Rich with a sprinkling of fair musk-rose blooms:
And such too is the grandeur of the dooms
We have imagined for the mighty dead;
All lovely tales that we have heard or read –
An endless fountain of immortal drink,
Pouring unto us from the heaven's brink.

John Keats (1795–1821)

On His After-Fame

And now the work is ended, which Jove's rage,
Nor fire, nor sword shall raze, nor eating age.
Come when it will my death's uncertain hour,
Which of this body only hath a power,
Yet shall my better part transcend the sky,
And my immortal name shall never die.
For, wheresoe'er the Roman eagles spread
Their conquering wings, I shall of all be read;
And, if we poets true presages give,
I in my Fame eternally shall live.

Metamorphosis XV
Ovid (43 BC–AD 18)
Translated by George Sandys (1578–1644)

Sonnet 60

Like as the waves make towards the pebbled shore,
So do our minutes hasten to their end;
Each changing place with that which goes before,
In sequent toil all forwards do contend.
Nativity, once in the main of light,
Crawls to maturity, wherewith being crowned,
Crooked eclipses 'gainst his glory fight,
And Time that gave doth now his gift confound.
Time doth transfix the flourish set on youth
And delves the parallels in beauty's brow,
Feeds on the rarities of nature's truth,
And nothing stands but for his scythe to mow:
    And yet to times in hope my verse shall stand,
    Praising thy worth, despite his cruel hand.

William Shakespeare (1564–1616)

Blow, Bugle, Blow

The splendour falls on castle walls
    And snowy summits old in story:
The long light shakes across the lakes,
    And the wild cataract leaps in glory.
Blow, bugle, blow, set the wild echoes flying,
Blow, bugle; answer, echoes, dying, dying, dying.

O hark, O hear! how thin and clear,
    And thinner, clearer, farther going!
O sweet and far from cliff and scar
    The horns of Elfland faintly blowing!
Blow, let us hear the purple glens replying:
Blow, bugle; answer, echoes, dying, dying, dying.

O love, they die in yon rich sky,
    They faint on hill or field or river:
Our echoes roll from soul to soul,
    And grow for ever and for ever.
Blow, bugle, blow, set the wild echoes flying,
And answer, echoes, answer, dying, dying, dying.

Alfred, Lord Tennyson (1809–92)

Index of First Lines

Index of Authors

Making a Difference

the children's charity

All the royalties from the sale of this book will go to the children's charity NCH.

NCH works with children, young people and their families to help them sort out problems. We've been around for more than 130 years. Here are some of the things we do:

- NCH supports young carers - young people the same age as you who have the tough responsibility of looking after a sick parent or sibling

- NCH goes into schools to help stop children truanting and being excluded

- NCH helps young people cope and offers help and advice when parents separate

- NCH finds young homeless people somewhere to live

- NCH helps make sure that young people who are disabled get to have the same opportunities as other young people

- NCH finds foster homes for children and young people who are in care

- NCH helps young people who are getting into trouble to sort out their problems

- NCH helps young mums and dads to cope with being a parent.

NCH has projects all over the UK. Wherever you are, there will be an NCH project nearby. If you want to find out more about NCH, you can go to our website at: www.nch.org.uk/whatever